Pots

Harriet Rycroft
Photography Andrew Maybury

bloom
gardening · nature · inspiration

Contents

03

Grow / p64
Discover the best
plants for pots in
all seasons

04

Care / p124
Learn to support
your plants and
help them thrive

Introduction

If you will stay close to nature, to its simplicity, to the small things hardly noticeable, those things can unexpectedly become great and immeasurable
Rainer Maria Rilke, *Letters to a Young Poet*

Beware! This is a highly addictive form of gardening.

A long time ago, when my husband and I bought our first home – a one-bedroom ground-floor flat in London – one of the first things we did was to buy a couple of green plastic tubs. I filled them with cheap and cheerful perennials and put them in our front garden. Immediately the place looked owned, inhabited, loved.

I knew next to nothing about plants in those days, but I liked the colours of the flowers, and soon I needed more plants... and then I needed more pots. The hobby snowballed. I studied horticulture while my children were small and then became a professional gardener, spending many years in sole charge of the garden and display areas of Whichford Pottery in Warwickshire, makers of hand-thrown terracotta flowerpots. My task was to inspire visitors, and so I created seasonal displays of pots overflowing with every kind of plant I could beg, buy or propagate, whether it was recommended for containers or not. Every week brought new lessons in keeping the plants happy through heatwaves, gales, frosts and downpours. Customers began to ask for my advice and I began to give talks and write about my work. I have been talking about it ever since.

My incurable flowerpot habit has a long heritage – people have been growing plants in pots for thousands of years. All over the

Previous page My hens are named Margery, Susana and Vita after some of my gardening heroines **Above left** I relish the fact that by the time autumn arrives quite a lot of our house has disappeared **Middle and right** My yard is my gardening playground and laboratory and I use pots to create a garden where there is almost no access to the soil

world potted plants enhance outdoor living spaces, whether they are punctuating the grounds of stately homes or standing on humble city doorsteps to welcome guests. It seems to be a very basic human need to surround ourselves with greenery, and pots raise and frame plants, allowing us to notice details that would be lost in the hurly-burly of large flowerbeds. Gardening in pots brings the natural world in miniature to your doorstep: when spring sunshine arrives you'll find ladybirds trundling to and fro on the rim of a pot and wrens hopping among your plants looking for tiny caterpillars; in the heat of summer you might spot a frog cooling its belly in the compost beneath a hosta – each season has its delights.

More than 30 years after that first purchase I am still gardening in pots, partly in clients' gardens but also for myself in the concrete yard at the back of our family home in the Cotswolds. In this yard I use flowerpots – hundreds of them – to create a garden where there is no access to soil. Unfortunately we also have to park the car there; if we didn't I would have filled the whole space with containers!

You don't have to plant hundreds of pots. A single pot on a table, a pretty window box or a cluster squeezed on to a balcony is enough to make a home look loved. Most of us don't have lots of spare space or time, so although I'm not going to oversimplify things I'm going to avoid much of the advice I've found to be unnecessary and focus on things I've learnt through trial and error over decades of container gardening. You may disagree with some of my methods, and you are welcome to. What I do know about the complex art of horticulture is that questions rarely have a single correct answer and gardeners often stifle their own creativity by worrying about 'doing it wrong'. I hope that my experience will help you to experiment and play, and also to develop your own routines and techniques to suit your style and site.

This book concentrates on gardening in outdoor pots with ornamental plants, although edible plants do creep into my displays. My style (dense, intricate, lots of foliage and a few flowers) plays out in a shady yard where weeds are rarely pulled and never sprayed. It all pleases me but may not please others, and that's fine. I sometimes plant in other styles for other people. The world of horticulture is occasionally guilty of taking itself too seriously, so I like to reassure people that they can have garden gnomes, fairy lights and stripy petunias galore in their pots if it makes them smile.

Whatever style of container gardening you choose, the pastime provides stress-relieving side-effects in these challenging times and I heartily recommend that you wander out to check your pots for a few mindful moments every day. In caring for your plants and for yourself you will find that noticing is everything; you will start to register the slight droop of a thirsty leaf almost before the plant does, and little by little you will become a better gardener and a more contented person.

Above I like to use containers to create a relaxed jumble of plants **Right** A pot of *Carex conica* 'Snowline' and *Chionodoxa luciliae* (glory of the snow) on a garden table

01

Learn
Understand the art of planting in containers

A garden in pots

It's been said of Ginger Rogers – the dancer best known for her partnership with Fred Astaire – that she did everything the man did, only backwards and in high heels. As a container gardener, you will be following the same basic principles of ordinary, in-the-ground gardening, but you may face a few extra challenges along the way. This is largely because the plants are strictly confined and depend on you to be ready to notice problems and to intervene. With practice your show can be as spectacular and effortless-looking as Ginger's performances.

WHY GROW IN POTS?

When approached and undertaken thoughtfully, gardening in containers will make the environment around your home more hospitable for both people and wildlife. It gives you a chance to express yourself, reinvent your style and to experiment with new plants, colours and combinations. There are plenty of other reasons to garden in pots rather than in the ground.

The rose and honeysuckle on the fence are growing in the ground; placing pots in front extends the planting area on to the concrete yard. When the rose is in flower I move the pot of pinks in front. The self-seeded *Alchemilla mollis* and terracotta pots hide the plastic tubs

- You can garden where there is no access to earth in paved yards and patios and on balconies and roofs, and reap all the benefits of a garden, including the cooling effects of plants in a space where hard surfaces reflect and radiate heat.
- A collection of containers can baffle both noise and wind, making an urban space quieter and calmer.
- If you are new to gardening it is a good place to start, not because it is easy, but because it is limited. Looking after a few pots is less overwhelming than trying to tackle a whole garden or even a single flowerbed.
- If you are renting you can take your plants with you when you move.
- If you move into a new-build house (where the soil has often been wrecked by builders or paved over) you get quick, portable results with a few pots.
- You can bring plants close to your house without their roots causing insurance problems or interfering with drains and damp-proofing.
- Well-placed pots can frame views, provide focal points or create a friendly welcome. They can bring a welcome distraction from a blank garage wall or boring paving stones and can be used to hide ugly features such as downpipes and manhole covers.

All of the plants on this side of the gate and fence are in pots; I like to create flowerbeds with them, extending the garden into the yard and changing the layout when I feel like it

- Containers may be used to direct people, perhaps discouraging them from parking cars or from walking into a private area. They can also draw attention to an entrance or entice people to explore along a path.
- Plants that wouldn't suit your garden site and soil may do better in pots where you have better control of the growing medium, moisture levels and positioning.
- Pots can be moved to different parts of your space to take better advantage of seasonal changes, such as winter light through the branches of a tree, or warmth and light reflecting from windows and walls.
- Tender plants can be kept in pots, making them easy to move and protect in winter.

- Containers can house a plant collection that would get lost or muddled in a flowerbed.
- New plants for your garden can be tried for a season or a year in pots so that you can observe their habits before you decide where to give them a more permanent home.
- Fragrant plants or edibles such as herbs can be grown near the house for easy smelling and picking. They can also be raised up, away from rain splash and from the attentions of dogs and cats.

My fern collection lives in pots arranged in the shade of walls and of other potted plants

PLANTING IN POTS VS THE GROUND

Plants in pots depend entirely on you – on the growing medium you choose and the inputs you give them – so you must pay a little more attention to watering, nutrients (see fertilisers on page 136) and the positioning of pots.

In the ground, a plant that needs water can, to a certain extent, send its roots questing through the soil; while in moist ground a plant that hates to be waterlogged may survive because the plants around it are using up excess moisture and keeping the soil structure open. Both of these scenarios are much less likely in pots. The limiting factor for most potted plants comes down to water supply. Even if you live on the rainy side of Rainsville, you cannot rely on rainfall, especially when the plants have matured enough for their foliage to cover the surface of the pot (their leaves will act like an umbrella and hardly any moisture will reach their roots). Even in a large container they are unlikely to survive without any irrigation. And yet, if there is no drainage hole in the pot to allow excess water to escape, or if the drainage hole is blocked, the roots may drown. Unhelpfully, the symptoms of dryness and waterlogging are often the same – wilting and yellowing of leaves or leaf drop – so you must monitor the moisture levels in the compost.

All gardeners are used to looking at the topgrowth of plants in order to identify them and to judge whether they can tolerate cool or warm conditions, but you will find yourself thinking about roots almost as much as shoots. This is because a plant in the ground in a hot position can send its roots to cooler depths, but in an exposed container, especially one with thin walls, there is no escape. Equally, plants described as absolutely hardy may suffer in pots during winter if their roots are too wet, too dry or frozen and thawed too often. They all depend on you to understand their preferences and put them in the right place so that they can perform well.

Right plant, right place

Observation is the key to success: watch to see how your plants grow, how they relate to each other and what signs of distress they show so that you can step in before it is too late. Very few plants are irreplaceable so don't be afraid to experiment with plants and positioning. If a planting doesn't succeed or some plants die, don't leave them there looking miserable and crispy as a reminder of your mistakes – take the pot away, rescue the survivors and add any corpses to the compost heap, then have a little think about what went wrong and try again. To avoid further mishaps, do your research and select the right plant for the right place. The great thing about pots is they are relatively easy to move if you've got the position wrong, and sometimes just sheltering one pot with another is enough to solve the problem.

PLANT RESEARCH

Whether you're buying plants online or from a nursery, each should come with a description. A good plant description will give you a fair amount of information, but you may need to do additional research. Aim to check at least two sources, especially with online research, because some writers may present themselves as an expert on a certain plant, but in reality they may never have grown it.

Plants behave differently in different locations, so to research flowering time, eventual size, rate of growth and hardiness use a source that is referring to a similar climate to the one you live in. There really is no substitute for seeing a plant growing well and talking to the person who grew it, so visit specialist nurseries and gardens (and talk to gardeners on social media) to get the best growing tips. Photographs can vary wildly in their representation of flower colour so look at a few images if you're after something specific – I always spend time doing this when I'm deciding which new seeds or bulbs to buy.

Remember that the information on plant descriptions and labels usually refers to plants grown in the ground. Grown in a pot, a sunny-position plant may actually appreciate a little bit of shade at the hottest part of the day, while another may grow faster than it might in the ground – be ready to adapt. Here are some key things to look into.

Name Always research using the full botanical name to get the most accurate results. Don't let the dreaded word 'Latin' put you off. The botanical names are just names that are used all over the world to pinpoint exact plants – the more accurately you can identify a plant, the more you can find out

about its needs. Relying on common names can be misleading, as a common name can be different in another region and mean different things to different people.

Lifespan Confirm whether the plant is an annual (flowers and dies in its first year), biennial (flowers in its second year, then usually dies) or perennial (will live for more than one year); do note that some plants are short-lived perennials, so won't go on indefinitely. These categories can be a little fluid: for example, some bedding plants are described as annuals, but they may be short-lived or tender perennials that won't survive cold temperatures.

Hardiness Will the plant survive winter outdoors (referred to as hardy) or will it need some protection? Some common terms (such as half hardy or frost hardy) can be confusing; the terms I use are hardy, borderline hardy and tender (see pages 66 and 138–142). Consider these in the context of the local climate and the aspect of your plot before deciding if a plant is right for you.

Position This refers to a plant's requirement for sun or shade, as well as its ability to withstand other environmental conditions. For example, some plants require a sheltered position protected from cold winds and hot sunshine.

Sun-lovers such as this *Arctotis × hybrida* (African daisy) need to be at the front to avoid being shaded by the house or by other plants

Begonias and plectranthus are happy tucked in the shade of the huge *Tetrapanax papyrifer* (Chinese rice-paper plant) leaves

My pelargoniums often start the summer on this sunny wall before being moved to lower positions as the days get longer

This south-facing wall is a warm spot for sun-lovers; the shade of the house creeps across in the afternoon to cool them down

Flower and interest Look for a long-flowering season and consider what else will be up at that time. If the season is short, does the plant compensate by having striking foliage? Does it have interesting berries or seedheads? Or textured or coloured stems?

Ultimate height and spread When grown in containers, some plants will not become quite as big as the height and spread indicated on the label, as this suggests their final size when planted in their ideal site and soil in the ground, but the information is still important. The speed at which they reach their ultimate size is also important because they may shade out other plants or need potting on soon.

Habit Does the plant remain tall and narrow or does it spread, cascade or climb? The answers will affect which containers you use and which plants you may combine it with. Different varieties and cultivars of the same species can vary enormously: for example, some petunias will cascade vigorously, whereas others will form meek, rounded clumps.

You can position plants more densely in containers than you would in the ground

Pruning This usually applies to woody plants and some climbers, and is worth checking so you can make a note of timings.

Planting distance Most often given for bedding plants and bulbs, this information is a recommended density for planting a number of the same plant in the ground. Take it with a pinch of salt; experience will tell you what you can get away with and what

density pleases you. You can generally plant much more densely in pots, especially if the plants are only going to be in position for a few months.

Planting depth This is most often given for bulbs. It can usually be taken as approximate depth, but can be important for some bulbs such as autumn-flowering *Nerine bowdenii,* which likes to be planted with its neck sticking out of the soil surface. It will also give you an idea of how deep a pot you will need. A few other plants (such as grafted roses and clematis) will do better planted with their crowns (where the shoots join the roots) below the surface of the compost and will need a deep pot. Most plants should not have their roots buried more deeply than they were in their previous home.

Soil If a plant needs damp conditions, it is likely to prefer a generously sized container and you must be confident that you will water it regularly enough. If you are not a very consistent waterer or your site is hot and windy, look for phrases such as 'drought-tolerant' or 'well-drained soil'. Note if it is an ericaceous plant, you will need ericaceous (acid) compost.

Warnings Plant labels will only sometimes give warnings about toxicity to animals and humans. If you are particularly sensitive (or have curious pets), it's best to put in the research to avoid accidents.

Choosing plants

The question you should always ask yourself when you browse for plants is not, *Can I grow it in a pot?* – (yes, you can grow practically anything in a pot) – but rather, *Does it earn its place in a pot?* Does the candidate have a long season of interest? Does it flower repeatedly? Is it evergreen? It gets extra points if it has interesting foliage, smells wonderful or has colourful stems or berries. Indeed, I would say that foliage is the most important qualification for many plants because it lasts much longer than flowers.

If you're struggling to make a plan, choose one plant you love and which will tolerate the conditions you can give it, then place other plants with it to see if you like the effect. You can do this in a trolley at the garden centre. From this small beginning, the rest will follow. Just don't fall into the trap of having one of everything as this can make your pots look more like a stamp collection than a garden. Repeating plants as well as colours and shapes ties a display together and is more satisfying to the eye.

FIND INSPIRATION (MINDFULLY)

Do have a look to see what other people are doing, but social media, magazines and TV shows can all conspire to make you think your pots should look perfect all the time. They won't! Don't forget that some pictures may have been styled, there may even be some fakery, and that published photographs represent a moment chosen to show the planting at its best, before the rain broke the stems or snails ate the flowers. All the pots in this book live in my yard and I have deliberately avoided any special styling so that the photographs show real life.

Visiting public and private gardens is a great way to fuel your creativity. You may see stupendous displays, but these are often only possible with

Pelargonium 'Frank Headley' provides just as much interest with its foliage as with its flowers

Try making a monochrome arrangement – it'll make you think more carefully about form, texture and foliage

A green tapestry of contrasting foliage shape and colour lasts longer than flowers; *Persicaria runcinata* 'Purple Fantasy' is in the centre

extensive glasshouses, or a behind-the-scenes growing-on area, or a team of gardeners, or all three. Sometimes, especially where money is no object, fresh arrangements are swapped in frequently and fading plants discarded. By all means take inspiration, but don't let the pursuit of perfection spoil the joy of growing. Try not to beat yourself up by comparing your efforts to others; just think about ways of making your space your own and enjoy the process.

CONSIDER YOUR COLOURS

Choosing a colour scheme is a useful place to start. For example, when I'm deciding which bulbs to plant in the autumn for my spring displays I start with a colour palette: I might opt for hot oranges and reds, or choose refreshing blues, whites and yellows. Often I will use one colour scheme in one set of pots and go for a different scheme around the corner. I always think about foliage and stem colour as well as the flowers.

Looking for links between your plants (and pots) can be a starting point for colour combinations. Finding harmonious repetition will encourage your eye to move around the planting. For example, a nemesia with two-tone flowers (such as *N.* Aroma 'Plums and Custard') might inspire a purple and yellow potful. Or the hints of violet in the leaf veins of *Coleus* 'Campfire' might pair well with the deep purple leaves of *Phormium* 'Platt's Black'.

Your eye automatically forms connections between similar colours, so the red of these tomatoes picks up the red of nearby flowers

Play with pot colours as well as plants: two-tone *Nemesia* 'Lady Lisa' connects the blues in the glaze to the pink of the petunia

Tying plants together with attention to detail enhances them all. Combinations can also support each other: the dark red flowers of *Dahlia* 'Bishop of Auckland' tend to disappear in the garden, but teaming them with *Canna* 'Musifolia', which has green foliage edged with a red line, makes the bishop sing (see page 40).

You may prefer to mix colours randomly, though I warn you this can have quite a monotonous effect (rather like mixing all the colours of modelling clay together makes a disappointing brown), and plumping for a set of colours makes selecting your plants easier. I tend to choose two or three colours which I match carefully, then I may relax and let something else creep in to liven it up.

INDULGE YOUR MOODS

The beauty of growing in pots is that you are free to create a particular atmosphere or style and then change that whenever the mood takes you. It's possible to create a formal, structured look using topiary and architectural plants, or achieve a cottage-garden style with an unruly melange of flowers, shrubs and edibles. Instead of a full-size meadow, create a naturalistic feel using shimmering grasses and annuals, or grow a woodland on your patio by using trees in tubs. It's all eminently achievable with the right choice of plants and pots.

I let a flouncy collection of plantings (based on pink, white and pale yellow flowers) engulf the bench – next year I will choose a different look; in other parts of the yard I have used reds and oranges

Changing the style of your display doesn't necessarily mean a whole set of new plants each season. I keep most of my perennials (both hardy and tender) from year to year and enjoy the challenge of making the space look slightly different, perhaps by moving plants into different pots, or by combining them with fast-growing annuals or bulbs.

Sometimes I use a completely artificial theme exploiting both the appearance and the names of plants. One year I made a spring display with the theme of a louche night out (using *Tulipa* 'Jackpot', 'Global Desire', 'Night Club' and so on). It's not likely that people noticed the link, but it kept me entertained.

BE RESOURCEFUL

Containers focus attention on your new green friends, so that even ordinary plants become extraordinary as you notice the curl of a tendril or the frilled edge of a petal, so there's no shame in using affordable 'patio plants', such as gazanias and petunias in summer or primulas and violas in autumn and spring. A lot of these widely available bedding plants (colourful, fast-developing plants used in temporary seasonal displays) are popular simply because they are reliable performers. Most people use them just for one season, but some (for example argyranthemum or the zonal pelargoniums, often sold as geraniums) are in fact perennials and can be kept and reused.

Simple summer bedding plants allow you to experiment with colour without spending a lot; this petunia is in the Frills and Spills series

A bird's eye view shows that the potted birch trees at the end of the house connect with my neighbour's trees

Using free plants takes a lot of pressure off when you're experimenting – you'll feel less afraid of killing them. I grow anything I can get hold of in my pots, including cuttings and divisions of plants taken from friends' gardens or swapped with neighbours. I also make use of the self-seeded forget-me-nots that grow like weeds in my garden, as well as random tree seedlings – oak, beech, hazel, holly, hawthorn

– which I incorporate into tiny potted landscapes. Small tree specimens can be potted on into bigger pots as they grow, and birch, acers and many conifers will tolerate life in a pot for years if you feed them.

THINK BIG

Don't just focus on filling the surface of your pots – there is lots of space above them and around them, just waiting to be colonised. If you have enough room for big containers it's possible to grow quite large trees, shrubs, climbers and perennials. In summer, dramatic dimensions can be reached with fast-growing annuals such as *Tithonia rotundifolia* (Mexican sunflower), *Ricinus* 'New Zealand Purple' or

25

Cosmos bipinnatus Sensation series, as well as tender perennials such as *Salvia confertiflora* – these can be much more exciting than the compact plants that are commonly recommended for pots, and can transform your space.

As your plants grow they cast more shade so you may have to swap pots around, moving sun-lovers further apart and nestling shade-lovers beneath the canopy. If you find that plants in a mixed planting are getting shaded out by beefy neighbours, either dig them out and plant them elsewhere or prune the bigger plants – sometimes just removing a few large leaves or some lower branches is enough to let the light in.

If you only have room for small or medium-sized pots (or you have a balcony with a weight restriction) there are slow-growing or dwarf varieties of many garden plants, some bred especially for container gardening. I absolutely love pine trees and have one or two would-be large ones in tubs (such as a 2m tall *Pinus roxburghii*, which in theory could reach 50m), but I also have a few dwarf varieties which have been quite happy in pots for years.

PLANT FOR WILDLIFE

Newsflash: your back yard does not solely belong to you. A major joy of growing plants is that we can also create oases for wildlife. This is not

Pines and other evergreen trees and shrubs form the backbone of my potted displays all year; the display is fleshed out by seasonal flowers and foliage, as is the case with these daffodils and tulips

just a matter of trying to do no harm but of taking positive action. Start by encouraging pollinators with a diverse range of flowers that bees, hoverflies and butterflies enjoy throughout the year, including autumn (try the sputnik-like blooms of *Fatsia japonica*) and winter (hellebores, crocuses, irises). It's easy to find useful flowers for spring and summer, but as a general rule opt for single or semi-double flowers, rather than double, as these are more likely to provide nectar and pollen. And always avoid buying plants and bulbs treated with neonicotinoid pesticides (ask the supplier for assurance).

Single and semi-double flowers (like this seed-grown dahlia) are best for pollinating insects

Dense cover and a range of heights of trees and shrubs encourage visits from birds, and I often stand at the kitchen window watching dunnocks, wrens and blackbirds inspecting my potted plants. One spring a whole clutch of blue tit fledglings emerged from the eaves of our house and dropped into my containers, where they waited for their parents to gather aphids from potted shrubs and trees (birds make for brilliant natural pest control). You're less likely to get charming scenes like this if you worry about aphids and therefore spray insecticide about.

Insects such as ladybirds also rely on plants for cover, especially in the winter, and dense evergreen plants such as conifers will help. Of course plants provide food for some insect larvae too, but a few missing leaves is a small price to pay to have the magnificent elephant hawk moth caterpillar living in your fuchsias.

By all means keep your container garden tidy if you like it so, but do keep an undisturbed and untidy corner nearby where a few stacked pots and some plant debris will provide cover for beetles, frogs and hedgehogs. Bumblebee queens sometimes tunnel down in pots to hibernate – if you find one, just pop the plant back in its pot and leave it until spring, when she will fly away.

Planting in pots

When it comes to settling your plants in their new potted homes, you will help increase your success rate year after year by being observant, making notes and taking photographs. My top tip is to record what you have put in your pots, especially the names of bulb varieties and how many you put in. It will help you to see if they have all come up as expected and to make the displays better each year. Labels in pots are useful, but may fade or get mislaid.

POTTING UP

When I was working at Whichford Pottery, the question I was asked on a daily basis (after, *Where are the toilets?*) was: *What size pot should I use for my new plant?* I wish I could give you hard and fast rules but the truth is that there are too many variables. Bear in mind these principles and learn from experience.

- Choose a pot big enough to allow at least a few centimetres around the current rootball, giving room for root growth into fresh compost on the base and around the sides. I allow a minimum of 2cm all the way around the sides for a rootball that's up to 20cm diameter, or 5–6cm for a bigger one. If it is a vigorous, fast-growing plant, give it more space.
- Shake or gently push the compost all the way down the gaps with your fingers. Be careful not to leave any big spaces or to squash the compost down so hard that all the air is squeezed out. The top of the rootball should end up 2–2.5cm below the rim of the pot to allow for watering. Any lower and the plant looks sunken (and you are wasting precious space), any higher and compost can gradually wash out of the pot, exposing roots to the elements and wasting water.
- The plant should not be buried much more deeply than it was in its old pot.
- Think about how big the plant is likely to get in the upcoming growing season: as a general rule, the foliage can be twice the volume of the pot, any more and the plant may tip over or dry out quickly; it might also look out of proportion.
- When you pot up new or young plants as a single planting (one plant in a pot), don't be tempted to upsize too much; a plant that outgrows its pot can be potted on into a bigger pot, but a small plant in a big pot can look odd and could even decline in health in stale compost.
- You can usually upsize generously in spring when vigorous growth starts, but avoid this in autumn/early winter, as you don't want a plant spending a cold season in a mass of wet uncolonised compost.

Don't pot plants on into much bigger pots; the blue pot will suit this pelargonium for summer

A healthy rootball emerging from a pot, which has a big drainage hole covered with a crock

- Perennial climbers such as a rose or a clematis require a different approach, as once they have started growing up a support (such as a trellis) they are hard to repot without causing damage or cutting back very hard. Give a plant like this a pot that will suit its ultimate size. You can plant other plants with it to make sure the compost does not stay soggy and become stagnant, then gradually remove those once the climber's roots are well-established.

A NOTE ON THE DRAINAGE LAYER

As long as your pot has drainage holes there is no need for what's commonly known as a 'drainage layer', no matter what size of pot you are planting. It is much more important to use good, quality growing media (see page 60) and to put the right plant in the right place and the right pot. A layer of crocks (broken pots) or gravel does not improve drainage; in fact there is some evidence that suggests it impedes it, because water does not move easily from a fine material to a coarse one. In my experience a drainage layer simply reduces the volume of compost available to the roots of the plants. The large spaces may be colonised by slugs, and, worst of all, when you come to tip the plants out of your pot all the crocks fall out, tearing plant roots and making a mess. Simply cover the drainage hole(s) loosely with a crock or two to stop compost from falling through the holes while the planting establishes.

SINGLE PLANTING

Keeping a single type of plant in a pot (rather than mixed planting, which is planting different plants together in one pot) is the simplest approach to container gardening. It makes bringing tender plants under cover for winter straightforward and you can change the look of a group by moving individual plants in and out of the display. Some plants are also easier to manage in splendid isolation for the following reasons.

Nuisance neighbours Some plants may batter more delicate companions with sharp-edged foliage (large varieties of phormium and grasses such as miscanthus), or elbow them out with vigorous growth (some of the larger canna varieties and bamboo). Those with vigorous fleshy roots (agapanthus, hostas) can fill a pot quickly and out-compete other occupants. And those with strong, wiry roots (some ferns) can make very dense rootballs that can't be penetrated by companion plants.

If you want to add such a plant to mixed plantings, one option is to plunge the whole pot into a bigger one (so that most of the roots are confined), and plant around it. Another option is to place one pot on top of the other. My oldest trees and shrubs don't have room to accommodate other plants in their pots, so I put pots of vigorous spreading plants that tolerate some shade (ivy, for example) on top to utilise the space.

To stop the plant in the small pot from rooting into the big one, place a piece of slate tile under the smaller pot.

Fireworks I think of some plants as fireworks, giving a brief burst of colour and then sinking back into obscurity. This is fine in a herbaceous border because when, for example, your lupins or delphiniums have finished flowering, it is easy to hide their scruffy foliage with something else. This isn't so easy in a pot. My approach is often to plant the one-hit wonders by themselves and to move them to a less prominent position once they have performed. I do this with roses, putting them on display only when they are in flower. If you don't have room to put plants out of sight, you will have to love them enough to put up with their off days.

A brief season Spring bulbs such as narcissi, muscari and tulips are a must-have, but many of them have a relatively brief season. You can either plant them as single plantings and move them away when they have gone over, or mix them with other bulbs and/or plants that have a longer season of interest. I almost always go for the single pot option for summer bulbs which don't repeat flower or have foliage that looks unattractive as it dies back, such as *Acidanthera murielae* and lilies. I prefer to grow these in tall, narrow pots that can be slotted in between other pots as they come into flower.

The potted fern *Woodwardia unigemmata* sits on the surface of a pot of *Fuchsia* 'Lady Boothby', so that its huge fronds can cascade

I keep *Rosa* 'For Your Eyes Only' in a plastic pot and bring it out when it is flowering; I then disguise the pot with more decorative ones

For protection I keep the fragile or less easily replaced bulbous plants (such as special snowdrops and roscoea) in single pots to avoid losing or accidentally damaging them when they completely disappear while dormant. Many sun-loving plants also dislike being overshadowed and will give up the ghost in a dense planting, for this reason I keep perennial dianthus (pinks), sedum, hylotelephium, sempervivum, some species of pelargonium (*P. × sidoides* 'Burgundy') and many tender succulents as single plantings, or at least with like-minded plants that are not too floppy or greedy for light.

MIXED PLANTING

Combining plants in one container to make a beautiful plant community is one of the creative pleasures of having pots. Just as in nature, the plants exploit various niches, so your plant choice can reflect this: tall, vigorous sun-lovers provide shelter for creeping or spreading plants that like to thread their way in and out of shade; a climber could be encouraged to ramble among other plants or to clothe the bare stems of a shrub or tree; and trailing plants can flow over the edges and help to keep all the roots cool. As with any planting, think about colour, texture and form. You can also focus on the details, and have fun matching the colour of one flower to the tiny stamens of another, or putting fine foliage next to large leaves to emphasise the scale of both.

Only part-fill the container with compost to make positioning plants (largest first) easier; make sure the plants have the same needs

When creating mixed plantings in autumn you can add bulbs (in this case tulips) between and beneath other plants

When combining several plants in the same container, remember they need to enjoy similar conditions in terms of climate, aspect and water availability in order to thrive happily together. But even if you haven't seen a particular combination recommended, give it a go. I recently planted sweet pea 'Cupani' with my 'Black Opal' tomatoes – they both enjoyed my sunniest site, a large pot, plenty of water and a few doses of fertiliser, and the sweet peas happily scrambled up the same support the tomatoes were trained on. Perhaps I didn't get as many flowers or tomatoes as I might have if I had dedicated a big pot to each, but they looked good together for the whole summer.

If you are going to go to the bother of creating mixed plantings make sure you don't do things by halves. Fill your containers generously and make them earn their keep – it is easier to take a plant out of a mixed planting and give it a new home than it is to establish a newcomer among neighbours which have already settled in.

Try to make best use of the space above, around and inside the pot. If you have a large, deep container you can use specimens with large rootballs and fill around them with smaller plants. You can cram plants fairly tightly into such a pot because the roots will plunge into the depths of the pot. Make sure the surfaces of all the rootballs

There's nothing better than seeing early crocuses pushing through mixed plantings in late winter

are at the same level because if one is higher than the others, irrigation will wash compost off its surface and expose roots, which will eventually die. The bigger the container, the easier it is to construct and maintain a mixed planting, but the principles can easily be scaled down to pots that are only about 20cm in diameter and depth.

There is a balance to be struck between overcrowded and sparse planting. Over time, you will get to know the growth rate of the plants you favour and how they develop over the season and will find complementary plants that don't overwhelm each other.

SEASONAL MIXED PLANTINGS

Using hardy plants to create mixed plantings that could last several years is a sensible approach, but I find creating seasonal mixed plantings more exciting. There are two main planting times for these: autumn (October and November) and early summer (when there is no risk of frost in late May and early June). Emptying and replanting containers is quite a big job, but with good plant choices you shouldn't need to do this more than twice a year. You can create a planting in autumn to last for six or seven months and then dismantle and replant your pot in early summer for colour and life until the first frosts... and so the cycle continues. For inspiration on what to plant, see pages 38–41, page 66 and the plants in the Grow chapter.

Summer to first frosts Mixed plantings can be made out of hardy plants or tender shrubs, perennials, annuals and bedding plants in the warmer months. It is easier not to mix hardy and tender plants, as when the first frosts arrive you'll know which plantings need protection and which can stay outside without having to be dismantled. Growth will be fast in summer so pay attention to ensure some plants don't engulf others.

Autumn to spring Autumn is a rewarding time of year to devise mixed plantings of trees, shrubs, perennials and bedding plants because you can

A just-potted mixed summer planting; the plants will soon start to knit together and overflow

By autumn, some summer mixed plantings are so voluminous that their pots become invisible

also stuff the plantings with spring bulbs. These little packages of potential are easy to insert among the plants and reliably give bursts of colour from February until the end of May. Even the drabbest of days is brightened by the sight of crocus shoots piercing the frozen compost, and from then on there is a crescendo of colour.

Mixing bulbs and plant types does take a bit of planning but it's an enjoyable puzzle. You could keep it simple with single plantings (put tulips in one pot, daffodils in another and crocuses in another), but if your pot is large enough you can put all three together and add plants on the surface. Position the bulbs at the depth each type requires, and position surface plants above the lowest bulbs (usually tulips); smaller bulbs, such as crocus (which only need to be a few centimetres deep), can be inserted between the plants. The bulbs' shoots will find their way between and through all but the densest rootballs. Choose plenty of evergreen plants to give some presence through winter and pay attention to the colours of their foliage and stems for best effect. Their shapes and textures will play a big part too, especially when outlined with frost.

This was a mixed summer planting of dahlias, bedding plants and tender perennials. I started by cutting down the dahlia stems to better see what was left and pulling out the bedding plants I didn't want to keep. Tender plants were dug out with as much of the rootball intact as possible, and potted up for overwintering under cover. I dug up the dahlia tubers last, shook the compost off them and set them indoors to dry

DISMANTLING
MIXED PLANTINGS

At the end of summer If you want to keep and reuse some of the plants in a large summer mixed planting, use a sharp trowel to cut around their roots and lever them out. Start at the edge and take the smaller plants out first, it will make it easier to judge how far out and down the roots of the larger plants have spread. Don't be afraid to cut through some roots but try to leave enough to support the plant. Smaller pots can be carefully tipped out so that you can pull the plants apart. If you want to keep tender plants over winter, dig them out before the first frost hits and pot them up into the smallest pot their roots will fit into.

At the end of spring When your bulbs are fading and your bedding plants are running out of steam, decide whether you are going to empty your pots or keep them going for next year. I empty out most of my mixed plantings at the end of spring simply because I want to free up my biggest pots for summer planting. I also love to use tulips and most of them won't be worth keeping. To do this, I dig out all the surface plants and (if they aren't going to be on display) I pot the perennial ones up in plastic pots and hide them in a shady corner behind the greenhouse. Rejects are thrown on the compost heap.

Spring bulbs that you want to keep require a bit more attention. One

option is to wait for the foliage to die, then dig up and dry off the dormant bulbs. Pop them into paper or netted bags, label them and keep them in a cool garage or shed for replanting in the autumn. You might find that when you dig your tulips out they have split into smaller bulbs; these will not flower next year and aren't worth reusing, so focus on the ones that have formed nice big bulbs. These can be replanted in autumn.

If you have smallish pots of smaller bulbs (narcissi, scilla, crocus) you can either dry off and store the dormant bulbs, keep them in their pots (keep them fairly dry while they are dormant) or plant them out in the garden. If they are not dormant yet, I plant the whole potful out as a clump; if they are dormant or nearly so, I pull the clump apart into an irregular shape so that the bulbs will look more natural when they come up the following spring.

Keeping a planting intact Give pots you are keeping intact a liquid feed or two while the bulb foliage is green, cutting it back only when it yellows. Deadhead, trim or remove bedding plants and generally keep the pot tidy. Depending on the plants used, the pot may benefit from a slightly shadier position for the summer. Don't overwater these pots or the dormant bulbs may rot. Narcissi, muscari and crocus are likely to flower again the next year, but tulips are less reliable.

Planting combinations / Spring

↑
5 *Narcissus* 'Sailboat'
2 Yellow *Viola × wittrockiana*
10 *Chionodoxa luciliae* 'Alba'
1 *Acorus gramineus*
'Variegatus'

↓
10 *Bellevalia pycnantha*
'Green Pearl'
1 *Bellis perennis*

↑
1 *Sorbaria sorbifolia* 'Sem'
1 *Uncinia rubra*
1 *Leucothoe* 'Little Flames'
10 *Tulipa* 'Parrot King'
20 *Narcissus* 'Toto'
6 *Viola* 'Amsterdam'
25 *Muscari* 'Superstar'

→
10 *Tulipa orphanidea*
(Whittallii Group) 'Major'
15 *Muscari* 'Siberian Tiger'
2 Purple *Viola × wittrockiana*

←
Small trough
5 *Tulipa* 'Blue Beauty'
12 *Narcissus* 'Elka'
9 *Muscari* 'Joyce Spirit'
16 *Crocus* 'Whitewell Purple'
4 *Viola × wittrockiana*
   (Panola) 'White Blotch'

Large trough
9 *Tulipa* 'Blue Beauty'
10 *Narcissus* 'Lieke'
16 *Muscari* 'Joyce Spirit'
19 *Crocus* 'Whitewell Purple'
5 *Viola × wittrockiana*
   (Panola) 'White Blotch'

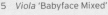

↓
1 *Chamaecyparis
   lawsoniana* 'Pembury Blue'
10 *Tulipa* 'Temple of Beauty'
10 *Tulipa* 'Antraciet'
15 *Narcissus* 'Hawera'
15 *Crocus tommasinianus*
   'Lilac Beauty'
1 *Hedera helix* 'Mein Herz'
1 *Thymus citriodorus*
5 *Viola* 'Babyface Mixed'

→
5 *Tulipa* 'Cape Cod'
10 *Tulipa* 'Hocus Pocus'
2 *Euphorbia* × martini
   'Ascot Rainbow'
1 *Carex comans* bronze-
   leaved
1 *Thymus pulegioides*
   'Archer's Gold'

Planting combinations / Summer

→
Combinations work well
when you take care to match
at least one key colour.
Here the dark purple of
Nemesia Aroma 'Plums and
Custard' is picked up by
Verbena 'Showboat Midnight'

→
Tomato 'Tigerella' is trained
around a metal obelisk, while
twining climber *Thunbergia
alata* 'African Sunset' is
allowed to scramble up the
obelisk and the tomato

→ →
Dahlia 'Bishop of Auckland'
stands out well against the
green-leafed *Canna* 'Musifolia'

Combinations / Summer–Autumn

← Close plant neighbours can reduce the need for staking. The stems of pink-flowered *Salvia involucrata* 'Boutin' may be floppy and fragile, but *Melianthus major* is giving natural support with its dramatic foliage

↑ Try combining dark blue, purple, maroon or black flowers with pale foliage to stop them from disappearing into the background. This is *Salvia microphylla* 'So Cool Purple' with *Senecio candidans* 'Angel Wings'

← Fast-developing summer plantings may include borderline hardy perennials, tender perennials, summer bulbs, bedding plants and plants grown from seed, including edibles. Try this mix: *Melianthus major*, chilli 'Black Hungarian', *Dahlia* 'Candy Eyes', *Chaenostoma cordatum* Abunda 'Colossal Blue', *Dichondra argentea* 'Silver Falls', *Fuchsia microphylla* 'Silver Lining' and *Senecio cineraria* 'Silver Dust'

02

Plan

Shape your space with the right pots in the right place

Practicalities

Most of us garden because we love plants and enjoy the process of looking after them – none of us wants to see our efforts wasted. A bit of thought about the practicalities involved and a good look at where you want to put your containers will save you from disappointment. Pots may seem self-contained, but they do have a context: your home, the outdoor space and even the wider landscape. They will always work better if you keep that context in mind.

ASSESS YOUR SITE

The first this to do is consider the space you are working with so that you can work with the conditions.

Climate The local climate will impact what you grow and how you treat your pots and plants through the seasons. Pay particular attention to minimum winter temperatures and maximum summer temperatures in your area (it's easy to check this online). If you find the plants you want to grow are not hardy in your climate, you will need somewhere to shelter them over the winter, such as a greenhouse.

The brightest place in our shady yard; early spring bulbs placed here are always the first to emerge. Warmth stored in the south-facing wall also helps borderline hardy plants to thrive

Microclimate The specifics of your plot will modify the climatic conditions significantly. For example, if your house is at the bottom of a hill you may be in a frost pocket, while buildings, fences, hedges and trees can all make rain shadows, meaning your containers will be inadvertently sheltered from the rain. Buildings surrounding your plot, together with hard surfaces, reflect and radiate heat, so you may find that a courtyard or patio stays surprisingly warm and allows you to grow more tender plants. If you live in a large urban area, you could also benefit from the 'heat island' effect, which means that average temperatures are a few degrees warmer than rural areas.

Wind We often want to place containers near buildings, in passageways or on balconies, but gusts of wind can bounce off walls and fences and swirl around corners, tipping containers over. Wind also makes plants transpire water faster from their leaves, even in shade, and this causes stress and makes them more likely to tip over as the rootball dries out. If you don't want to be woken by a crash in the middle of the night, choose stable containers and fill them with drought-tolerant, compact plants or grasses that don't need a sheltered position.

This sheltered corner faces north-east and is only touched by a little morning sun; acers, hostas and ferns are perfectly happy here

chilly afternoons, but also beautiful morning light, while a site open to the west can be exposed to rain and wind, but enjoy warm summer evenings. Don't despair if your garden faces north or is very enclosed; there are lots of hardy and beautiful shade-loving plants to use in pots.

Don't forget that the aspect will impact how you arrange a group of containers, as the pots to the south will shade the ones on the northern side, while the eastern side of a group may be sheltered from the prevailing winds. Indeed, aspect scales right down to individual pots: for example, you can tuck a shade-loving plant in on the northern side of a mixed planting sitting in full sun.

Aspect The direction your space faces will dictate much of your plant choice and influence the way you use your containers. Observe where the shade and shadows fall during the day and take photographs to remind yourself of the way this changes from season to season.

Every aspect has its pros and cons. Here in the northern hemisphere, a south- or south-west-facing patio will become very hot in the summer. This can make for floriferous summer displays (if you pay attention to the watering), but it will also heat the sides of your pots, so it would be prudent to avoid metal containers. A plot facing east can mean cold winter winds and

Is there a water source nearby? However artfully placed your containers are, they won't look good if they are so far away from a tap that nobody waters them. As well as an outdoor tap, consider installing a diverter and water butt attached to a nearby downpipe to harvest rainwater.

What is the surface like? Consider whether there is enough hardstanding for your containers. Sometimes a pot can make a focal point in a flowerbed but it isn't a good idea to put pots directly on grass or soft ground because the drainage holes may get blocked or they may absorb too much water from the ground during winter.

Soften the appearance of a paved passageway with a few pots, but be careful not to block access or create trip hazards

Vigorous roots can even escape into the soil and pin your container down permanently! You can use bricks or paving stones to keep pots off soil and grass, but it can be fiddly to mow around them.

Rain will splash dirt from smooth surfaces such as concrete or paving on to the sides of the pots, so if that bothers you keep the area swept.

Rain splash won't be as much of a problem with gravel, but you may not like the seedlings which will pop up (of both weeds and desirable plants) and you won't be able to sweep up dropped leaves or compost easily. Containers may leave marks on decking or paving stones, so think about using pot feet to minimise this.

Will your pots be in the way? You may need to move containers to get access to manhole covers, meters, pipes or other essentials. If you are in a block of flats or using communal areas, check any regulations – be sure you are not blocking access for emergency services, maintenance workers or fire exits.

Is there space to work? If you have more than a few pots, your life will be a lot easier if you have a nearby working area. A bench or table to work at is very useful, and somewhere to store spare growing media and fertiliser, a few tools and a wheelbarrow or sack trolley. Compost bins and a greenhouse are ideal components of a garden's engine, but not all of us have room for those.

Are you safe? It sounds dramatic, but do look after yourself: be careful lifting (use a sack trolley or ask for help), don't leave trip hazards lying about (such as the hose) and don't rush around. Sturdy footwear is a must, as even a small pot can break your toe if dropped.

Containers

Your mission, should you choose to accept it, is to provide a container filled with growing medium that's big enough to house the plants' roots plus room for them to grow outwards and downwards. The roots, growing medium and container together must be of a strength, size, shape and weight great enough to anchor the plant so that it does not fall over or blow over, even when it's on the dry side. The only other essential is drainage holes. You may need to drill new or bigger holes, so consider if the material (or your tools) allow you to do this. Make the holes as big as you can without weakening the base; ideally you can at least push a thumb or a trowel handle through the hole of medium and large containers.

STYLE

Planting style is easy to change from year to year and I'm certainly not going to dictate how things should look in your garden, but it's unlikely you'll want to buy a new set of containers frequently. Think about what sort of containers would suit your space and reflect your taste. Sleek, modern containers might be at odds with a country cottage. Ornate urns could look twee against a

The pots that look like beaten copper are really made of plastic. One sits on a drain cover because it is light and can be easily moved

contemporary house. A barn conversion might cry out for a few converted water troughs, while an allotment might be enlivened by an upcycled wheelbarrow. You might wish to throw out the rule book and create something eye-catching, ironic or completely your own.

It is almost as easy to fall in love with a pot as it is with a plant, but I like to achieve some sort of unity in style and/or colour in each area. Consider the colours and textures already present in the surrounding hard landscaping and plants, then decide whether you want your containers to blend in or stand out. Perhaps your garden furniture or the plants themselves feature a colour that could be picked up by the containers. Of course you may prefer an eclectic look, but even this works better by design rather than accident.

POSITIONING

Containers can enhance the design of your garden when placed in a way that leads the eye. They need to relate to their surroundings and to mean something, rather than look like someone has just plonked them down.

- Pots will feel intentional in groups, so try clustering a few pots around a bench or at the end of a path.
- Containers lend themselves to formal structure; rows or pairs of pots can

Vary the height and shape of the pots, but repeat colours and plants for a cohesive display

The Belfast sink is very heavy but small pots and light tins are easy to move around

frame gates and entrances, but don't fall into the trap of placing a pair of pots at every doorway and bend of a path, or your garden may start to look like a show-jumping course.

- Before you go shopping, place an object such as an empty dustbin or cardboard box that is about the size of the pot you want in the space you are considering, then look at it from every angle. If it's a pot you already have, move it to the new position and live with it for a few days before planting.
- This may sound obvious, but put your pots where you can see them. Containers dotted around a garden are not only harder to look after, but if you can't see them regularly your effort and expense will be wasted. This is especially important

in winter when you may rarely set foot outdoors. And remember that window boxes are not just for passers-by, so include some fine detail to interest you as you look out as well as brighter colours or bolder shapes for neighbours to admire.

GROUPING

If pots are the punctuation marks of the garden, groups of containers can form whole paragraphs and it can be great fun to gather pots of different shapes and sizes together, perhaps raising some up on bricks, crates, steps, walls or tables to give an impact greater than the sum of their parts. Groups can give your winter and spring plantings (when the plants tend to be smaller and more slow-growing) much

Small, vintage flowerpots such as these are lovely but dry out quickly and do best in shade

You can make a pot look taller by raising it up on a plinth made of bricks

more impact, especially if you repeat colours and shapes from pot to pot.

Don't automatically put all of the tallest pots or plants at the back. Try to make a landscape rather than a carpet and tinker with the combinations of height, texture and colour until you're happy that the display hangs together. As the plants develop you can tweak the positions, perhaps pulling them a little further apart. Plant aficionados may enjoy displaying collections this way – perhaps cacti, auriculas or ferns – even creating outdoor shelving units or 'plant theatres'.

I keep my containers in large, fairly dense groups, especially in the summer. They dry out less quickly this way, because they shelter each other from the worst of the sun and the wind and create a more humid microclimate, which slows down transpiration from the leaves. I enjoy the way they knit together, but even quite a loose group will have a beneficial effect. I guarantee it will look better than spacing your pots out in a prim little row.

SIZE

As a rule, bigger containers are easier to look after than small ones because they hold a greater volume of growing medium and therefore of stored water and nutrients. A small pot will dry out faster than a large one. Volumes are deceptive and a pot that does not look much larger than its neighbour can have a much greater volume. (If you

These robust, glass fibre-reinforced, concrete troughs have been made to look like driftwood

The dustbins in my front garden are a long way from a tap so watering is infrequent; succulents are ideal for this exposed, west-facing site

are mathematically minded, measure the height, the diameter of the base and the top of two similar pots, then look up online: how to calculate the volume of a truncated cone.)

Of course the larger a container is, the harder it is to move (it's best to move it while empty, then plant it up in situ, which will save your back and allow you to see whether the plants suit the space as you position them). Other limiting factors are space and cost. Weigh up your priorities: if your heart is set on a beautiful, hand-thrown pot, you may need to settle for a smaller size; but if you want something more portable and utilitarian, a plastic one of the same size will be a fraction of the cost.

You do not need to spend a fortune on large pots. You can use plastic tubs, old wooden barrels, dustbins, removal crates, buckets – anything that allows drainage holes to be drilled in and is clean and stable. You can paint your found containers to match your scheme or cover them with hessian or woven willow, or instead of beautifying them, hide them under lots of plants (easier in summer) or simply put better-looking containers in front of them.

It's also possible to make medium-sized pots look larger by raising them on a plinth made of loose bricks or paving stones. Make sure this is very stable. Alternatively a cluster of smaller pots can do the job of one big one and you will just have to spend a bit more time ensuring that they are watered.

MATERIALS

The material from which your container is made can make a significant difference to your choice.

If you are putting containers on a balcony, roof garden or raised or exposed area (decking, steps, walls) check load-bearing capacity and any regulations carefully – you may need to opt for the lightest material possible and save the load for compost and plants. Make sure any containers are very stable, as these sites can be windy.

Front garden pots are sometimes tempting targets for thieves. It is possible to pin down more valuable pots with steel cables passed through the drainage hole and a metal ring inside the pot, which is then attached to a ground anchor, but for peace of mind I prefer to use heavy containers of no obvious value. My front garden currently hosts a group of planted metal dustbins of varying sizes. I think the big ones would be very hard to

Pots in clusters around a feature such as a bench look intentional and appealing

shift, but I also used bicycle locks to secure the handles to an iron bench.

Terracotta (unglazed) This material has been used to make flowerpots for at least 2,000 years. It is beautiful and characterful (especially if hand-thrown), and often develops an attractive patina with age. Good-quality terracotta should not crack or laminate in frosty conditions, but always ask the manufacturer, as sometimes a guarantee is offered. Terracotta insulates roots fairly well against extremes of cold and heat; its porosity has a cooling effect in hot weather. In my experience, plants in terracotta are not harder to keep irrigated (as is often suggested) as the plants' fine roots will cling to the wall

Large containers can be expensive, while repurposing a metal dustbin gives you plenty of volume for your money; it will be stable in a windy position but may need insulating if the site is sunny

of the pot – even in dry conditions a well-established rootball will not shrink away from the wall (as it does from plastic) and become hard to re-wet.

Glazed ceramics These have the advantage of a wide range of colours and finishes. Quality is variable and some may crack in freezing conditions, especially if made in countries where cold weather is not an issue. Dark-coloured pots with relatively thin walls can become very hot in direct sunshine. Stoneware pots are often robust and made with a wide variety of finishes, including salt glaze, which fuses to the walls of the pot giving a slightly dimpled texture. These pots do not have the porosity of unglazed terracotta.

Stone, concrete, cast stone

A weathered stone trough or urn is a desirable thing, but real stone planters are hard to find and expensive. They need positioning carefully as they are heavy and difficult to move. They are often quite shallow, so it can be tricky to find plants which are happy in them. Urns and planters made of cast stone or concrete can look almost as good, especially when they have weathered a bit and grown some moss. They can look a little out of place if they don't match the stone used for the walls of the house or garden. It's best to buy from reputable suppliers who can assure you the product is frost-resistant.

Polystone Polystone and polyterrazzo are a mixture of stone particles and resin frequently used to make contemporary planters with a smooth finish, rather like polished concrete or stone. These containers have the advantage of being relatively light.

Resin, fibreglass, fibrecotta There is a growing range of containers manufactured in these materials, often with a finish that looks like wood, metal or pottery. Fibrecotta or fibreclay is made of a combination of fibreglass, cellulose and clay. Various claims are made about the porosity and durability of these materials; they are generally strong, relatively light and hard to break, although some will crack if dropped or may have a coating that is easily scratched or chipped. They can be surprisingly expensive but very attractive.

Woven plastic bags Reusing bags such as builders' bags can be useful for workaday planting such as a crop of potatoes or tomatoes and can be put away when not in use. They are not generally recyclable and may shed fragments into the soil. The same kind of plastic is used to make hanging pouches, which can be tricky to keep watered, but make a handy home for fast-growing temporary plants. I use mine for trailing tomatoes such as 'Tumbling Tom'.

Metal Many metal containers offer good stability and are hard to break. The contemporary look of rusted

Upcycled galvanised containers are very useful; just ensure they have drainage holes

Corten steel and the vintage look of zinc-galvanised bins and tubs have been very popular in recent years. If used in an exposed position, consider insulating the sides of metal containers before filling with compost as the walls can become extremely hot or extremely cold, damaging roots and shoots. I use foil thermal insulation material for this; biodegradable alternatives are wool carpet underlay or old newspapers. Metal drinking troughs for livestock make excellent large planters. Old metal watering cans and biscuit tins are good candidates for upcycling too. You will need to use rustproof paint on the edges of any drainage holes you make in galvanised containers so the base does not rust.

Wood Wooden containers, such as square Versailles planters, have good insulation properties, and they can often be repainted to suit a colour scheme. Ready-made wooden planters raised on legs can be useful for those who use a wheelchair or garden while seated. The wood is usually pressure-treated to slow the rotting process but you can also line them with old compost bags. Half-barrels (most commonly available as cast-offs from the drinks industry) are very stable; the larger ones give huge volume-for-money, but they are very hard to move once full, so be sure of their position. These barrels are fairly long-lived, but they will eventually rot. They should not be left empty or dry for a long time as the wooden slats will shrink and fall out. I find barrels useful for long-term perennial plantings in a shady spot where they are unlikely to dry out.

Plastic The walls of plastic pots tend to be thin, providing little insulation and no porosity, they may become brittle and their colours may fade with age. They are light, which is an advantage for portability but not for stability. Manufacture and disposal of plastics is environmentally problematic but there is merit in reusing plastic tubs, barrels and pots before they are ultimately thrown away or recycled. I would urge you to avoid buying new plastic, which is derived from fossil fuels and adds to the world's problems at each end of its life.

A note on reusing plastic Like many gardeners I have a messy area beside my shed where I stack spare plastic pots and trays and random bits of junk that may come in handy one day. All of the plastic pots are reused over and over again, and they either came with plant purchases or have been rescued from friends. I use them for propagation, potting up young plants or holding plants that have been taken out of displays and are waiting to be used again. I also use the large ones for tall plants and trees, hiding them behind better-looking pots. There are various alternatives, such as pots made of coir, cardboard or starch, but I will reuse my collection until they are so broken that they have to be added to the recycling.

Jars and urns can have awkward shapes; place a pot in the neck of the vessel to plant into

SHAPE

The shape of containers obviously makes a difference to their style and their volume, and each shape has its uses and appeal.

Conical flowerpot The classic flowerpot is very practical – a vessel with a wider top than base is easy to fill and empty. If a pot is very flared, with a much narrower base than top, be aware that a top-heavy planting or a standard tree (such as a lollipop-shaped bay) will get blown over easily.

Jar-shaped This type of vessel looks very attractive planted up, but don't fall into the trap of planting a pot that has a neck much narrower than its body with something which has very vigorous roots because you will not be able to slide the rootball out and may find yourself having to either chop the plant up or break the pot in order to release it. Unless you are planting small bedding plants that will pull out easily at the end of the summer, it's best to place another pot in the neck of a ceramic jar and plant into that. Winter planting directly into ceramic jars isn't advisable because the damp rootball will expand when it freezes and become so trapped that it may crack the jar.

Urns Traditional pedestal urns can be spectacular but you need to be sure they are securely attached (the pedestal is often separate and the

Narrow long tom planters are very attractive but easily knocked over and broken

whole thing top-heavy) and that they have good drainage holes. They can be hard to plant if they are very shallow and, because they are usually placed by themselves on a wall or pillar, they need careful planting and maintenance as they tend to dry out quickly.

Straight-sided These containers, whether square, rectangular or cylindrical (including old chimney pots and dustbins) can be hard to empty; you may have to dig your plants out rather than tipping them out. A couple of years ago I thought it was a great idea to plant lots of *Canna* 'Musifolia' in plastic dustbins; this vigorous plant was so happy that it filled the bins tightly – when autumn came I had to spend hours hacking them out with a spade!

Large and small pots together will help you create a display with maximum interest

good drainage, making them useful for plants that detest waterlogging, such as some irises and lilies.

Shallow and wide Containers such as seed pans are good for spreading and creeping plants, such as many herbs and alpines, or for small, vigorous spring bulbs. They can remain very damp at the base, especially during the winter, so rarely suit anything that is very sensitive to waterlogging. Traditional seed pans often have several drainage holes for this reason.

Lips Containers with an internal lip (often found on contemporary plastic or resin containers) provide an excellent hiding place for slugs and small snails, so avoid planting snail food (salads, hostas) in them and top them up almost to the rim with grit to make them less welcoming. Containers with a very curved over external lip (many large plastic pots have this because it makes them stronger, as do some ceramic pots) are a favourite daytime roosting place for snails, so you will need to check them regularly to avoid your plants being shredded every night.

Square and rectangular These are stable and make efficient use of a small space; troughs and boxes pushed against the wall of a passageway provide good growing opportunities without blocking access. For windowsills, go for boxes with as much depth as possible to maximise the planting options and make sure they are securely fixed, especially on high windowsills.

Tall and narrow Tall planters and long tom flowerpots are useful in confined spaces and corners, but their small footprint also means that they may tip over quite easily and must be positioned and planted accordingly. Tall containers give room for trailing plants to reach their full potential and provide

Hanging baskets I rarely plant summer hanging baskets because these are the exception to my 'not every day' watering rule. By definition they are raised up in a relatively breezy position and so dry out quite quickly, especially as they are usually close to walls where they receive very

Culinary herbs stay clean in a hanging basket but will need careful watering

Use tough plants in summer hanging baskets, such as this *Lophospermum* 'Red Dragon'

little rainfall. This is a situation where water-retaining granules or gel may be helpful. I also experiment with techniques such as burying saucers at the bottom of the baskets to act as a reservoir but I am rarely happy with the results. I always insert a small, empty plastic flowerpot or a plastic bottle (cut in half and inverted) in the top so that I can water into this, which helps the water to percolate right into the compost rather than just wetting the top then running off the surface.

I do sometimes plant strawberries in hanging baskets as this keeps them away from slugs. Culinary herbs that appreciate good drainage and sunlight can stay cleaner when elevated, too. Baskets that are attractive in themselves and don't need to be completely hidden can be a good place to experiment with trailing and climbing plants such as lophospermum, *Thunbergia alata*, plumbago or some varieties of plectranthus. Sometimes the best hanging baskets are in shade, using plants such as trailing begonias and spider plants in summer, or ivy, cyclamen and heuchera in winter.

Growing media

Growing media – most commonly bagged potting compost or multipurpose compost in the UK – provide physical support and anchorage for plants. The compost must drain well, retain enough air spaces for the roots to have sufficient oxygen available and yet hold on to water and nutrients. It's quite a tall order! A reliable, easily available and sustainable growing medium is the holy grail of container gardening and I don't think we are quite there yet, but progress is being made.

CHOOSING A MEDIUM

Some composts work better than others, so you may need to try several brands, but always avoid peat-based products. It is better for delicate wetland habitats and for the world as a whole to leave peat in the ground where it stores carbon. If peat-free composts are not available at your local retailer, ask them to stock some.

Homemade compost Few of us have the resources or time to make our own potting compost, although it is an art that has not died out and some people make their own mix using ingredients such as topsoil, leaf mould and garden compost from their compost heaps. This is certainly the most sustainable answer and can give good, if possibly uneven results. Garden compost or soil

at the top of a container can give a crop of weed seedlings, while proprietary (shop-bought) composts should be relatively sterile, containing neither weed seeds nor pests, and should give predictable results. Using garden soil by itself in pots is best avoided as it tends to become too compacted for healthy root growth.

Bagged compost Growing media you can purchase may be based on peat, coir, bark or wood waste, composted municipal waste, sheep's wool or bracken, with varying proportions of fertiliser, sand, grit or loam (graded, sterilised topsoil) mixed in, but the description on the bag is usually pretty vague. Always shop for peat-free, but be mindful of other ingredients – coir (waste material from coconut production) also has environmental issues, not the least being that it is shipped enormous distances. Unless you are a very specialised grower of unusually sensitive plants, a peat-free, multipurpose compost will usually meet your needs.

If the compost in your bag contains a lot of large wood pieces or even fragments of plastic, alarm bells should ring – such poorly produced compost can have extremely variable nutrient levels, and plants may 'sit' without growing as they should.

The colour of good compost should be dark brown, almost black. Its texture should be friable and it should be fine enough to pour between plants without leaving large gaps between lumps. The particles should vary in size and shape – a completely dust-like or silt-like compost will settle into a solid mass and your plants will not be happy for long. When you squeeze a handful of a good, open-textured compost it should feel spongy, sticking loosely together and breaking apart again easily. It should feel slightly moist but not wet. Dry compost can be a respiratory hazard whereas very wet compost may become stagnant and encourage fungal disease in your plants. If the compost you have bought is extremely dry, spray water on it to damp down the dust. The compost should smell fresh and woodsy, not sour or mouldy.

I like to use a proprietary compost which contains some loam as it seems to hold on to nutrients effectively. John Innes composts are a range of mixes that traditionally contain loam, grit, peat and varying amounts of fertiliser, and are often recommended for container planting, especially of shrubs and trees (peat-free versions are now available). I don't use John Innes mixes by themselves as they tend to become quite compacted in pots, leading to poor root health; I mix them with ordinary multipurpose to keep the compost structure open.

Bulb fibre There is absolutely no need to use bulb fibre for outdoor planting. This is a low-nutrient growing medium (spring bulbs do not require extra fertiliser to flower well in their first year of planting) which causes a great deal of confusion; gardeners are often led to believe that it is essential. Bulb fibre is usually sold in small bags and is much more expensive than multipurpose compost; it usually contains charcoal to keep the compost from going stagnant because it is really designed to be used for forcing bulbs, growing them indoors in pots which may have no drainage holes at all.

Compost additions If the compost you have is very claggy, sticky and likely to turn into a solid mass when wet, add grit, perlite, leaf mould or composted bark to keep the compost's structure open, which is particularly important for plants that demand good drainage and for winter plantings.

If you do add one of these ingredients, apply it generously and mix thoroughly. To make an appreciable difference the mix will need to be about 60 per cent compost and 30–40 per cent of your chosen ingredient.

I rarely add anything to my compost, except sometimes grit for some succulents and bulbs (such as *Iris reticulata*). And I use perlite for seeds and cuttings. Perlite is a heat-expanded volcanic rock and is light and porous but stable. It keeps the growing medium open, crumbly and aerated. Always avoid inhaling the dust from perlite, and damp it down before handling. It's a finite (though currently plentiful) resource and high temperatures are required to make it. I have not found a good substitute so I continue to use it, but try not to waste it. Vermiculite has similar properties though it crushes more easily than perlite and holds on to more water.

I don't use composts that contain additives to retain water, in my opinion they are not good value for money and are only usable in summer. And I am sceptical about many of the products and media marketed for different plants, although I do use ericaceous compost for lime-hating plants that demand a low pH growing medium, such as camellias and blueberries. I find that ensuring pots are the right size, have good drainage holes and are placed in a position that suits the plants is more important than compost additions.

Composts for seeds and propagation
If you're propagating by seed or cuttings, the compost needs to be free-draining, as very young plants are sensitive to waterlogging. The growing medium must be free of large lumps or big fibrous pieces so that seedlings and newly rooted cuttings can be teased apart without breaking their roots, so if your compost is not

I mix perlite into my compost to keep it crumbly and free-draining for cuttings and seed sowing

fine enough sieve it with a garden sieve. Seedlings and cuttings may also be damaged by excessive amounts of fertiliser, so for propagation don't add fertiliser or use composts that boast high nutrient levels.

Specially formulated seed composts with an open texture and low nutrient levels can be useful, but I simply use my favourite multipurpose compost with a generous helping of perlite thoroughly mixed in. When you prick out seedlings into separate pots and pot up rooted cuttings, use normal multipurpose compost.

STORING COMPOST
Make sure stored compost is out of direct sunlight and sheltered from

rain. Even if it is packaged in sacks, the small perforations in the bag will gradually lead to wet compost if left outside. Heat or excessive moisture will cause compost to degrade. I store mine stacked on a wooden pallet in the shelter of a big tree, and cover it with a tarpaulin. If you have easy access to a large shed or covered storage area and plant a lot of pots it is definitely worth sourcing compost that can be delivered in large dumpy bags rather than plastic sacks. I reuse most of my plastic sacks for overwintering plants such as cannas or stuff them inside each other to use as winter insulation but the amount of plastic used still worries me.

If your compost has been in a large stack the bag may be flattened and feel very solid. This is not necessarily a problem – if you shake the bag, banging the bottom of it a few times on the ground, its contents should start to loosen up. If it is firmly stuck together and you have to break up every bit of it manually or with a spade, you might want to try a new brand next time.

When buying compost in person, avoid a product that has obviously been sitting for months, its packaging fading in the sun, as its nutritional content will have degraded.

REUSING COMPOST AND COMPOSTING

Even peat-free composts are not without environmental impact.

You can make efficient use of your compost by reusing it in the bottom of larger pots unless you have had problems with a disease such as tomato blight, or a pest such as vine weevil. I always add fertiliser and chop it up and stir it with a spade, because it may have become quite depleted and compacted, then I use fresh compost in the top of the pot, around the roots of new plants. If I know that the compost has already been reused a couple of times, or if it is full of roots or its structure has broken down, I add it to my garden composting heap or sometimes directly into my garden borders.

Spent plants, prunings, deadheads, any vegetable waste all go in my composting heap and bins. Even if you only have a small garden or yard, composting as much as you can and returning it to your beds helps to keep your soil healthy and to lessen the impact of your gardening on the planet. More and more ingenious composting systems for small spaces, such as hotbins and wormeries, are becoming available. The compost I make with my heap and bins usually all gets used in the garden borders, but I sometimes use it in the bottom of large pots. If you want to do this you must use very well-rotted garden compost, because if it is still breaking down it may mean that fewer nutrients are available to your plants and it will subside as it rots, so your plantings may sink down.

03

Grow
Discover
the best plants
for pots in
all seasons

How to use this chapter

There is a vast number of plants that are wonderful in pots, and it just isn't possible to list them all in this book. This selection is intended to create a reliable starter kit: if you choose something from each section you will have the beginnings of a plant collection that will give your pots colour, texture and form all year. If you're starting out, I would recommend that you avoid mixing hardy and tender plants in the same pot, just to keep things simple, then as you become more confident you can make your own rules. See pages 31–35 for planting single and mixed plantings.

Choosing a few plants from the first five sections: Hardy Shrubs and Trees, Hardy Perennials (inc Grasses), Hardy Bedding and Filler Plants, Alpines and Compact Plants, and Spring Bulbs will make a display that lasts from autumn until early summer, but may look a little quiet later in the summer. That's where the Tender Perennials, Summer Bulbs, Summer Bedding and Annuals sections come in, bringing summer colour until the frosts of autumn arrive.

All of the plants have been chosen to give a long season of interest and/or to flower reliably for a good length of time. Heights given are approximate, as the height and spread of a plant in a pot may be different to the same plant in the ground. Bear in mind that some plants will grow more vigorously in pots if they are happy (especially when newly planted), others will grow tall and weak if they're not getting enough light, and some may even become a little stunted if pot-bound, dry or starved, so it's up to you to give them optimal conditions. You can limit the size of quite a few trees and shrubs by clipping or pruning and many other plants can be pruned or trained, so don't be afraid to experiment.

KEY

Ⓟ Ⓑⁱ Ⓐ   Perennial / Biennial / Annual

☙   Good for pollinators

Ⓗ Ⓑᵒ Ⓣ   These ratings apply to plants in pots in an average UK winter; also see pages 138–142:
- Hardy (*will survive winter outside*)
- Borderline (*may need some protection in winter*)
- Tender (*will need protection from frost*)

☀ ● ◑   Sun / Shade / Part-shade

🌢   Evergreen

Hardy shrubs and trees

When transferring trees and shrubs from one pot to another, make sure they are planted to the same depth as their previous pot; burying too deeply can kill many of them. Evergreen plants will continue to transpire water all year and can suffer from drought in cold, windy weather, as well as during the summer, so remember to water them. Here is a hard-wearing selection to give year-round structure, colour and form, plus a few flowers.

Acer palmatum / Japanese maple

These small-to-medium trees are grown for their spring and autumn leaf colour and there are many to choose from, including **'Katsura'** (in shades of gold and orange) and the dark red **'Bloodgood'**. It's best to buy an acer that's in leaf in autumn to judge the foliage colour. Keep them out of cold winds (especially the fine-leafed varieties such as **'Dissectum'**) as it can ruin their foliage and even kill them. Also avoid scorching sun. No pruning is needed as they naturally grow into elegant shapes, but if you need to trim a branch, do so in late summer or autumn to avoid bleeding.

Betula pendula / Silver birch ↑

Silver birch is a relatively shallow-rooted and tough tree which may reach 12m tall in the ground, but can be kept long-term in a large pot or tub, which will restrict its growth. Its slender trunk and light canopy mean that it is less likely to blow over than other trees. Nevertheless give it a pot or tub with a wide, stable base. I have several 3–4m specimens in tubs 40–50cm wide. It is also attractive as a shorter, multi-stem tree. Small fluttering leaves turn yellow in autumn. The young trunk is warm brown, turning silver with age. Only prune lightly and in early autumn. It gets extra pot-points from me as around 300 insect species are associated with it.

Conifers

Essential for winter structure, conifers are characterful all year. Buy them as small plants to save money and pot them on each year. They are excellent in mixed plantings, but don't let other plants grow thickly over or against them as the covered foliage will die.

This evergreen selection focuses on slow-growing varieties that have good form without the need for clipping, but even a young *Cupressus macrocarpa* **'Goldcrest'** (which could eventually grow to about 12m in the ground) is worth using as a young plant then turning into topiary. Larger specimens in pots by themselves are useful as movable screens, windbreaks or bold backdrops for spring and summer flowers. I particularly love *Cryptomeria japonica* **'Elegans'** (growing up to 3m in 10 years) which forms a feathery, upright tree that's bright green in summer with hints of coral in its gently drooping twigs, changing colour to a warm rust in winter. Here are some others to choose from.

Chamaecyparis obtusa **'Teddy Bear'** / **Hinoki cypress 'Teddy Bear'** This one is dark green, though new growth is paler and emerges like fern fronds. 1.5m in 10 years.

C. pisifera **'Boulevard'** / **Sawara cypress 'Boulevard'** Loosely conical with blue, slightly curly foliage; 2m in 10 years. **'Baby Blue'** has a more rounded silhouette; 50cm in 10 years.

Cryptomeria japonica **'Tilford Gold'** / **Japanese cedar 'Tilford Gold'** A characterful blob that's more pet guinea pig than tree, with green foliage that has a golden tinge. Useful in the front of a group of pots. 50cm in 10 years.

Pinus densiflora **'Low Glow'** / **Japanese red pine 'Low Glow'** Develops a windswept look as it matures and its needles have a yellow tinge. Two other pines worth noting are dwarf *P. × densithunbergii* **'Jane Kluis'**, with rounded sprays of green needles, and *P. sylvestris* **'Westonbirt'**, which has thicker, bluish needles. All have attractive buds and candle-like growth in early spring. 50cm–1m in 10 years.

Thuja occidentalis **'Rheingold'** / **White cedar 'Rheingold'** Forms a fat, fluffy cone that's yellow in summer and coppery in winter. 1m in 10 years.

T. plicata **'Whipcord'** / **Western red cedar 'Whipcord'** Almost unrecognisable as a conifer. A little tuft of green when very young, but as it matures it sends out curved, scaly branches cascading over the edge of its pot. 60cm in 10 years.

Top left *Cryptomeria japonica* 'Elegans'
Top right *Thuja plicata* 'Whipcord' **Bottom left** *Pinus densiflora* 'Low Glow' **Bottom right** *P × densithunbergii* 'Jane Kluis'

Cordyline australis /
Cabbage palm ↓ →

(P) (Bo) ☀ ◐ ◌ ◊

This star-shaped plant is a bit of a container-gardening cliché, but so useful for long-lasting structure. Try blending it in with wispy, taller plants rather than doing the Victorian thing of plonking it in the middle of a ring of bedding plants. The green-leafed type is the hardiest (pictured below), while brighter-coloured cultivars such as **'Red Star'** or pink-striped **'Charlie Boy'** (pictured right) may need some shelter from the coldest weather. *C. australis* slowly forms a trunk (up to 20m in the wild) as it gets older, which gives it a tropical look, but most plants available to gardeners are young and about 40cm upwards.

Fatsia japonica 'Spider's Web' /
Japanese aralia 'Tsumugi-shibori' ↗
(P) ❋ (H) ◐ ● ◊

I find this plant's large-scale, variegated, evergreen foliage useful for brightening a dark corner and it can look beautiful combined with dark foliage or white flowers with a green or yellow cast, such as *Tulipa* 'City of Vancouver'. Mine has been in a large pot with *Luzula nivea* for several years. Autumn flowers are white and useful for late-flying insects. Very hard frosts and cold wind may damage newer growth (it will reach up to 1.5m). There is the green **F. japonica**, which is faster-growing and ultimately larger. × **Fatshedera lizei** (tree ivy) is a cross between *F. japonica* and *Hedera helix* (common ivy) and is sprawling with dark green, glossy, palmate foliage. × **F. l. 'Annemieke'** has yellow-

green blotches on its leaves; place its pot against a shady wall and, with a bit of support, it can climb to about 2m.

↙ *Hydrangea macrophylla* / Hydrangea

'Miss Saori' is a mophead hydrangea with double, pale pink flowers in summer, each petal edged with darker pink, set off by reddish foliage. It grows to 1m so is easy to keep in a pot, but if you have room, larger cultivars are worth trying too. Blue-flowered varieties tend to turn dusty pink unless in ericaceous compost and watered with rainwater. **'Zorro'** has dark stems and lacecap flowers in blue/pink (pictured bottom) and **'Tricolor'** has handsome, cream-edged foliage with white and pink/blue lacecap flowers (both 1.5m). For all *H. macrophylla* forms, wait until the leaf buds are near bursting in spring before trimming away old flowerheads as they give some protection against late frost damage. Prune to the next pair of strong buds below the old flower and avoid cutting too many branches back hard as these hydrangeas flower on the previous year's growth. Those sold in flower in winter and spring are forced and can struggle to adjust to outdoor life, so buy from nurseries rather than florists. These are thirsty plants; it is easier to keep them well-watered when they are grown in large pots by themselves and not placed in full sun. Use a high-potassium feed from spring into summer.

Ilex aquifolium / Common holly →

(P) (🐝) (H) ● ◐ 🌢

Hollies are suitable for pruning into
lollipop-shaped standards or any other
shape that takes your fancy. Named
varieties are either male or female,
so make sure you have at least one of
each if you want the red berries. Try
'Argentea Marginata' (female, pictured
top) for green and cream young foliage
tinged with pink. **'Silver Queen'** (male)
has darker green leaves edged with
cream. **'J.C. van Tol'** (F) has dark
green, less spiny foliage. Plain old
I. aquifolium, the British native species,
is a handsome plant, although you won't
know if a seedling is male or female
until it is a few years old.

Pittosporum 'Arundel Green' / Pittosporum 'Arundel Green' →

(P) (Bo) ☀ ◐ 🌢

With wavy-edged foliage in a pleasant
dusty green set off by dark stems,
this shrub can be clipped into a dense
dome or left to grow more loosely and
will reach about 2m. Best in a sheltered
position, especially when young. Other
varieties include **'Garnettii'** (grey-
green leaves with a pink edge, 3m),
P. tenuifolium 'Elizabeth' (grey-green
with a pink tinge in winter, 3m) and
'Tom Thumb', which is more compact
(1m) with dark, purplish leaves. All
are very useful as cut foliage for
flower arranging.

Prunus incisa 'Kojo-no-mai' / Cherry 'Kojo-no-mai'

A shrubby, ornamental cherry with pale pink, single blossom in early spring on bare, zig-zag branches. New foliage has a bronze tinge, changing to green, and finally orange in autumn. There's no need to prune, though you can do so lightly in summer, or choose to gradually remove lower branches to make a more tree-like form. Underplant with bulbs, such as the pink *Hyacinthus orientalis* 'Pink Festival' or *Crocus tommasinianus* and *Chionodoxa luciliae*. It will reach about 2m, but is slow-growing.

Sorbaria sorbifolia 'Sem' / Sorbaria 'Sem' ↗

This suckering shrub may be a nuisance in the garden but its fern-like, amber and lime-green foliage (which emerges very early in spring) can be appreciated in the confines of a pot. Split and replant every year or two. Pairs well with spring bulbs in similar tones such as *Tulipa* 'Parrot King' (as pictured above). Grows up to 1.5m in the ground, but usually less in a container (mine remains about 60cm tall).

Teucrium fruticans / Tree germander →

A rather gangly shrub that reaches about 1.5m; its stems and the undersides of its leaves look as though they are coated with silvery white felt. It is possible to clip it into a dense shape, but I prefer to leave mine loose, just snipping the odd branch to thicken it up a little. Expect lavender-blue flowers in late spring and summer; a good plant for a Mediterranean look.

Hardy perennials

Clematis / Clematis →

Perennial climbers can be tricky in pots because they may grow too large and can be hard to repot. However some large-flowered clematis hybrids, for example **'Esme'** in the **Boulevard** series (pictured), have been bred specifically to flower for a long season with a compact habit, clothing a 1–1.2m obelisk. Give them a pot at least 45cm wide and deep, and bury the rootball a few centimetres deeper than the pots they came in. Put in a sunny position, but use mulch and/or trailing plants to keep their roots cool. If you have large containers you can experiment with bigger clematis, but look for those that flower for a long season, such as *C. viticella* **'Polish Spirit'**.

Euphorbia × *martini* 'Ascot Rainbow' / Martin's spurge 'Ascot Rainbow' →

Handsome whorls of colourful leaves (yellow and green, flushed pink at the shoot tips) reach up to 50cm and bring warm colours to winter pots. In spring they terminate in chartreuse and green bracts enclosing tiny, dark-red flowers. The flowers complement practically any spring bulb. There are more discreet versions, including **'Rudolph'** (dark bluish-green, with dark red shoot tips). Note this is a short-lived perennial.

Ferns ↗ →

Ferns are best planted in individual pots; top-dress or pot on in late winter and cut off old/dead fronds if you want a tidier look – do this before the new fronds unfurl as they are quite fragile. Don't allow these plants to dry out. I look for evergreen and semi-evergreen hardy varieties. *Dryopteris wallichiana* (alpine wood fern, pictured top right) is elegant with striking dark stems, and *Polystichum setiferum* 'Pulcherrimum Bevis' (soft shield fern, pictured right) is one of the most beautiful and fluffy ferns. You can see it is handsome even at its least luxuriant in winter. *Asplenium scolopendrium* (hart's tongue fern) is glossy with crinkly edges and *Woodwardia unigemmata* (jewelled chain fern) has spectacular 1–1.5m trailing fronds that are bronze

tinted when young (keep in a sheltered spot). Deciduous ferns to try include *Athyrium niponicum* var. *pictum* (painted lady fern, pictured top left) in delicate shades of purple and grey.

75

Helleborus × hybridus / Hybrid Lenten rose ↗ →
(P) 🐝 (H) ● ◖ 💧

There are many colours and forms of hellebore with flowers from green to black via pink, white and yellow in late winter and early spring. In pots you can raise them up and see inside the nodding flowers more easily. Top-dress and feed in spring; hellebore roots are deep and greedy, so if they are coming out of the bottom of the pot it's time for a move into a larger pot. They can be used in mixed plantings for winter, especially while young, though they are eventually easier to keep by themselves. Pictured top right is **H. × *sternii* 'Silver Dollar'**, which has blue-grey leaves that look good all year, with flowers in pink-grey clusters (30cm). Bottom right is **H. × *hybridus* (Ashwood Evolution**

Group) in a very beautiful soft yellow. And pictured top left is **'Anna's Red'**, which is quite tall (up to 60cm) and a favourite for its vigour, wine-red flowers and marbled foliage.

Hosta / Hosta →

(P) (H) ● ◖

A classic subject for pots, hostas have bold, arching foliage that unfurls in spring. Many glaucous cultivars (such as **'Blue Moon'**, pictured) are more resistant to snail damage. **'Patriot'** has white and green foliage emerging from a purple base, **'Bedford Rise and Shine'** is a glossy green with acid-yellow margins, while **'El Niño'** is glaucous grey with white margins. Don't let hostas go short of water. Glaucous ones do well in more sunshine than the variegated or golden cultivars can take. Some will produce white or dusty purple flowers in summer.

Phormium / New Zealand flax

(P) (H) (Bo) ☀ ◖ ◆

There are many varieties of phormium, all feature bursts of glossy, strap-shaped leaves that contrast well with less structural plants. There are large ones that can grow leaves 2m long (such as **'Pink Stripe'**, with purplish-grey leaves) and will ultimately need a large tub to themselves as their roots are vigorous. And there are smaller options such as **'Golden Ray'** and **'Platt's Black'** (1m). Young plants can be useful verticals in mixed winter or summer plantings; they take a few years to start producing their longest leaves. As a general rule the more colourful they are, the less hardy, but once established most will survive all but the hardest UK winter. *Dianella tasmanica* (Tasman flax-lily) is a good alternative to phormium, as varieties such as **'Tasred'** (pictured bottom, green

leaves with red bases) and **'Destiny'** (pink bases) grow to about 60cm. Their clumps are easier to split too. Some may produce sprays of purple flowers in summer, followed by poisonous berries.

Grasses

Grasses contribute soft verticals and swaying movement to your plantings.

DECIDUOUS

Deciduous grasses don't necessarily disappear completely in winter, but they will look a bit scruffy so consider planting in separate pots for summer and autumn interest so you can move them into position when their fresh foliage is up, however they are lovely in mixed plantings too. Cut back in early spring just before growth starts.

← *Hakonechloa macra* / **Japanese forest grass**

   ● ◗

This forms beautiful, flowing, bright green clumps to about 30cm tall, becoming tawny in autumn. Excellent by itself or around the base of a tree or shrub. There are many golden and striped cultivars, the paler they are the more shade they need. Try **'All Gold'** or **'Stripe It Rich'**. Don't let them get too dry.

Milium effusum **'Aureum'** / **Bowles's golden grass**

Ⓟ Ⓗ ● ◗

Bright, golden blades will thread between other plants and pop up where they want to. Useful as a semi-permanent planting under shrubs or as a filler for spring plantings. Self-seeds.

Miscanthus sinensis / **Eulalia** ↑

Ⓟ Ⓗ

Choose the more compact varieties of this striking grass such as **'Kleine Silberspinne'**, which flowers in late summer/autumn. **'Morning Light'** is mainly grown for its foliage, which is edged with white and stands neatly upright. When mature either of these may reach 1.5m. **'Cute One'** is really small (40cm) with bronze flowers (pictured above). *M. nepalensis* also has beautiful golden, tassel-like flowers (1m).

EVERGREEN

All of these are useful in winter pots and look good all year. Comb them through if they start to look untidy, or snip out dead leaves or flower stems. If they become congested with dead growth, chop them back by about half, but do this in spring, just as growth starts, then feed, pot on or divide.

Anemanthele lessoniana / Pheasant's tail grass

Arching clumps of green and russet foliage become billowing clouds when the fine, long flower panicles emerge in summer; these are easily combed out when they have ripened. Easy in all but the wettest conditions, it is not always long-lived, but does self-seed.

Carex oshimensis / Japanese sedge ↗

Mounds of glossy foliage reach to 30cm. Try the striking **'Everest'** (pictured) or **'Evergold'**. Don't let them become pot-bound or dry as the tips go brown.

Festuca glauca / Blue fescue →

Fine bursts of blue-grey foliage (up to 20cm) have the best colour in full sun. Tolerates small pots and dry conditions. Sometimes produces airy grey panicles of flowers in early summer.

Luzula nivea / Snowy woodrush

Loose clumps of green foliage (up to 30cm) are edged with tiny silvery hairs. Flower spikes with white flowers rise above in late spring. Tolerates small pots and occasional dryness if kept in shade.

Stipa tenuissima / Mexican feather grass
Tufts of fine, pale green foliage (up to 60cm) become blonder and fluffier as summer progresses and flower spikes develop. Comb out the flower spikes in winter when they start to break and look untidy.

Uncinia rubra / Red hook sedge
Glowing, rusty red tufts of leaves make this small plant (up to 25cm) a good choice for contrast. It's only borderline hardy, so give it a sheltered position, especially when young.

Hardy bedding and fillers

This is a selection of hardy stalwarts used for filling gaps between large shrubs and perennials in winter and spring plantings. Some are useful all year, but will prefer a shadier position in summer; others are not usually worth keeping once spring is over. Bedding plants may be inexpensive annuals, biennials or perennials, usually sold in small pots or in multipacks and used as seasonal fillers. You can grow your own from seed or cuttings if you have room. Some herbs make good fillers too (see page 122).

Ajuga reptans / Bugle

Ⓟ ⚘ Ⓗ ● ◑ ◊

A creeping perennial with short spikes of violet-blue flowers in spring. Very useful in shade or beneath taller plants. **'Burgundy Glow'** (grey foliage splashed with cream and flushed purple), **'Braunherz'** (large, dark purple leaves) and **'Chocolate Chip'** (narrow, dark leaves) contrast well with green or grey-leafed plants.

Bellis perennis / Daisy →

Ⓟ Ⓑⁱ Ⓗ ☀ ◊

These are double forms of the common daisy better known as a lawn weed, and are short-lived perennials sold as bedding plants. White or pink flowers are held 10cm above neat green rosettes. For a hardy, tough, summer-flowering equivalent try **Erigeron karvinskianus**.

Erysimum / Wallflower →

Ⓟ Ⓑⁱ ⚘ Ⓗ ☀ ◊

In the UK, biennial wallflowers (*E. cheiri*) are strongly associated with kitchen gardens and Victorian-style bedding, but their flowers smell wonderful and I think they should be used more often in pots, especially with tulips in similar shades (mainly red, orange and yellow). They can be bought as small plants, but these are often compact varieties such as those in the **Sugar Rush** series. I prefer the old-fashioned, taller forms, which can be grown from seed or bought as bare-root plants in autumn. Firm them in well and feed them. Perennials such as **'Bowles's Mauve'** (purple flowers, pictured opposite left), **'Apricot Twist'**

(orange) or **'Red Jep'** (pink and red) develop a more woody framework and may flower sporadically through the winter, peaking in spring and continuing into summer if you deadhead. Perennial types aren't as fragrant as the biennials and may be short-lived, so take cuttings.

Geranium / Geranium

Not all hardy geraniums are useful in pots, but it is worth experimenting because many are fairly evergreen or don't mind being overshadowed by close neighbours. For example **G. pyrenaicum 'Bill Wallis'** produces small, bright purple flowers on long stems, which weave beautifully between tulips and may self-seed to make free fillers for next year. **'Dusky Crûg'** makes neat mounds of brownish-purple foliage, dotted with pale pink flowers in summer.

Hedera helix / Common ivy ↑

Look beyond the plain green or grey-variegated ivy often sold for hanging baskets (although useful) and you'll find some interesting cascading or climbing foliage, texture and colour. Try **'Parsley Crested'** (crinkly) or **'Mein Herz'** (heart-shaped, pictured above) – both develop brown tones in a cold winter. **'Luzii'** is lime-green splashed with bright green and **'Lalla Rookh'** is vigorous, with crinkly, dark green leaves.

Lysimachia nummularia 'Aurea' / Golden creeping Jenny

Creeping and cascading mats of golden foliage are topped with bright yellow flowers in early summer. May be a little scruffy in winter, but soon perks up as the weather warms.

Lamium maculatum /
Spotted deadnettle ↑

This low, creeping plant clothes the compost surface and trails over the edge of the pot. Short (10cm) spikes of flowers emerge in early summer. Cultivars include **'White Nancy'** (white flowers), **'Beacon Silver'** (pink, pictured above) and **'Pink Pewter'** (pale pink), all of which have silver foliage edged with green. **'Golden Anniversary'** has green leaves with a central silver streak and gold edges.

Myosotis sylvatica /
Garden forget-me-not ↑

With sprays of tiny blue, sometimes pink or white flowers that rise from overwintering clumps of leaves, this biennial will self seed in your garden and transplant easily in autumn. Alternatively, raise it from seed (sow in early summer for flowers the following spring) or buy it in packs as a bedding plant, though these will usually be cultivars of the more compact *M. alpestris*. *M. sylvatica* is taller and looser (to about 30cm), a great partner for tulips, it also thrives in shade.

Ophiopogon planiscapus 'Kokuryu' / Black mondo

Glossy black, grass-like straps about 20cm tall make this a distinctive plant. It spreads steadily, but you can also split it and squeeze pieces between other plants to make it look like it has spread naturally.

Trifolium repens / White clover

There are many trifoliums to try but **'Purpurascens Quadrifolium'** has been the most successful in my pots and goes well with spring bulbs. It's a creeping, four-leafed clover with dusky purple leaves that are edged with green. Fresh foliage emerges early in spring and white flowers in summer.

Viola × *wittrockiana* / Garden pansy

Bedding pansies are grown as annuals or biennials and planted out in autumn or spring. Their main flowering time is spring and early summer, but they produce large flowers sporadically through the winter too. Some have frilly edges and shaded colours, such as those in the **Can-Can** or **Frizzle Sizzle** series; others are a plain colour, often with a yellow eye, such as **'True Blue'** (from the **Matrix** series) or **'Padparadja'** (which is orange). Many are marked with dark central blotches. Bedding violas are derived from *V. cornuta*, and can be more long-lived than pansies. Their smaller

flowers usually stand up to wet weather a little better than pansies and some have a cascading habit. Many have markings that look like little faces, or their two upper petals may be a contrasting colour, or both. Try those in the **Sorbet** series, such as **'Tiger Eye'** (gold with dark brown veins) and **'Denim Jump Up'** (blue, pictured above). If viola plants are still strong but straggly in early summer, they may get a new lease of life if cut back hard and fed.

Throughout winter and spring, both pansies and violas do better in a sunny position, as they are prone to fungal diseases such as leaf spot when in damp conditions. They are good companions for spring bulbs; as the weather warms up into summer they will be happier in part shade. Deadhead regularly and remove badly diseased leaves.

Alpines and compact plants

Strictly speaking, alpine plants originate above the treeline of mountains. They are ideal for a small but light space or windowsill – introduce a few handsome rocks, perhaps a small conifer (see page 68) and mulch with grit to create a long-lasting, low-maintenance miniature landscape. Many mat-forming and compact plants are sold as alpines, but have less mountainous origins or have been bred for colour and vigour. They vary greatly in speed of growth so you may need to remove or split one if it starts to dominate. The more vigorous varieties can be used on the edges of mixed winter/spring plantings.

All the plants named here are easy-care and hardy evergreen perennials that suit a sunny site but there are alpines and mat-formers which are fine with part shade, such as *Leptinella squalida*, *Lewisia cotyledon*, *Sagina subulata* and many saxifrages, such as *S. stolonifera*.

Cushion-formers and tiny plants look attractive in small pots and seed pans for table-top displays or in the front row of larger groups, but alpines often have questing roots and may ultimately prefer a deeper container, such as a long tom pot or a Belfast sink. Note that some true alpines may require particularly sharp drainage and/or more shelter from winter rain.

For all plants listed: (P) ⚘ (H) ☀ ◊

Armeria maritima / Thrift
Round clumps of grassy foliage
decorated with small drumstick
flowers in pink or white in spring
and early summer. Try **'In the Red'**
or **'Splendens'**.

Aubrieta deltoidea / Rock cress
Innumerable cultivars of this spring-
flowering cottage-garden plant are
available, many in shades of purple,
but also pinks, blues and whites. Plant
where they can have at least one year
to settle and form a cascading cushion.

**Centaurea bella / Evergreen
cornflower** Grey foliage is joined by pale
pink, cornflower-like flowers in spring.

**Iberis sempervirens / Perennial
candytuft** An evergreen, mound-
forming sub-shrub with white candytuft
flowers in spring and early summer.
'Golden Candy' has golden foliage; give
it a little shade to avoid scorching.

↖ **Phlox subulata / Moss phlox**
Smothered in pink, white or purple
flowers in late spring, this alpine
creeps over the edge of a sunny
trough. Try **'Lilacina'**, **'Candy Stripe'**
or **'Snowflake'**.

**Sedum dasyphyllum 'Major' /
Corsican stonecrop 'Major'** ↗
Mats of blue succulent foliage
with white, star-shaped flowers in
early summer.

**Sempervivum tectorum /
Common houseleek** These succulent
rosettes are useful for tiny pots or
among stones and pebbles, which help
to stop birds from pulling them out
as they look for woodlice. There are
varieties in shades of blue, green or
red, such as **S. 'Terracotta Baby'**. Try
the webbed **S. arachnoideum**. These
are hardy, so don't confuse them with
tender succulents such as echeveria.

**Silene uniflora 'Druett's Variegated'
/ Sea campion 'Druett's Variegated'**
Vigorous, cascading mats of cream-
variegated leaves sprinkled with white,
bladder-campion-style flowers on short
stems in early summer.

Spring bulbs

Spring bulbs are my biggest garden extravagance – to me they make winter almost worthwhile. Most are planted in the autumn while they are dormant, however snowdrops, especially the named varieties, are usually sold 'in the green' during or just after flowering in late winter.

Most spring bulbs can be planted very densely, depending on the effect you want. Try not to place them so they are touching – if one rots then its neighbour is likely to suffer too – but it is possible to cram a surprising number into even a modestly sized pot. Just bear the size of the final flowers in mind: if they are large, you may want to give them a bit more space to allow them to open without crowding each other.

You can plant a single type of bulb in a pot and set it aside when the flowers have faded or you can plant several types of bulb in layers to create cheerful combinations and/or a longer flowering season. If you go for a mixed planting of bulbs, choose early, mid- and late-flowering varieties to extend the display, but be aware that the weather conditions can bring some on sooner than expected and hold others back, so be sure that you will like all of those colours together.

If you are planting multiple layers remember that they all have foliage as well as flowers, so plant them less densely than you would if they were by themselves, especially if you want to add plants on the surface (see pages 32–35). If you prefer you can plant bulbs in clumps, as you might in a flowerbed, rather than in layers across the whole of the pot, as this allows room for other plants or bulbs to expand. Be aware of each bulb's eventual flowering height to ensure any that are planted with shrubs won't be obscured.

Always take planting depths into account when choosing pots. Use a pot that is big enough to accommodate the ones that need to go deepest (often *Fritillaria imperialis* or tulips). A useful rule of thumb is to cover the bulbs with approximately twice their own height of compost. This means that the base of a large tulip bulb needs to sit 15–20cm below the surface, but they also need at least 10cm beneath them for their roots – so you should use a pot at least 30cm deep for tulips. If you would like to plant more than one layer of tulips, you may need an even deeper pot.

Here are the stalwarts that I use almost every year, but there are so many more to explore. For example, if you have large pots, try some of the big *F. imperialis*, camassias or alliums.

Top *Tulipa* 'Apricot Beauty' **Bottom** *T.* 'Candy Prince' and *Chionodoxa luciliae* 'Violet Beauty'

Chionodoxa luciliae / Glory of the snow ↑

Delicate but long-lasting starry flowers in shades of clear blue with white centres in mid-spring. (Note that *Chionodoxa* is now known as *Scilla*.) **'Alba'** has small white flowers and is a bit lax, but is lovely planted on the edge of mixed plantings; **'Violet Beauty'** is another option (both 12cm). Also look to *C. forbesii* **'Blue Giant'** and **'Pink Giant'**, which have very reliable, white-eyed sprays of flowers (15cm). *C. sardensis* has intense sky-blue flowers with a white centre (10cm).

Crocus / Crocus ↗

These and the irises mentioned on page 92 are valuable flowers for early spring pollinators as well as welcome signs of hope; their shoots often begin to pierce the surface before Christmas. The most commonly available earlier-flowering species, *C. tommasinianus* and *C. chrysanthus*, are usually short in stature (10cm) and it is easy to push their small corms in among plants; try *C. t.* **'Lilac Beauty'** and **'Whitewell Purple'**, as well as *C. c.* **'Blue Pearl'**, **'Romance'** (soft yellow with a dark base, pictured above) and **'Gipsy Girl'** (yellow with brown stripes). The slightly later Dutch types, derived from *C. vernus*, are a few centimetres taller and have larger corms. Their fat flowers may flop and become slimy when dead, so you may wish to pinch them off. Dutch types include **'Pickwick'** (purple and white stripes), **'Jeanne d'Arc'** (white) and **'Flower Record'** (purple). Watch out for mouse damage with all varieties.

Hyacinthus orientalis / Hyacinth

We are so used to seeing hyacinths forced for use indoors that sometimes we forget that they are perfectly hardy and lovely in the garden in mid-spring. Buy the ones that are not 'prepared' for indoor use and plant them fairly deeply, almost as deep as your tulips, with about 10cm of compost above them. This helps to stop them from falling over in full flower, as does planting them among surface plants. Even so, the heavy-headed ones may need some support – it is worth it for their rich colours and powerful fragrance.

Try **'Woodstock'** (maroon), **'City of Haarlem'** (creamy yellow), **'Splendid Cornelia'** (purple, striped) or one of the **Festival** series, which are multi-stemmed and have less dense flowers. All are approximately 25cm.

Iris reticulata / Early bulbous iris

Like the crocus, the miniature iris (about 12cm) flowers as winter turns to spring. You can put these in the edge of mixed plantings, but I like the way they look by themselves in smaller pots. They can then be raised up on a table so that you can see their intricate details; some are fragrant too. They need sunshine and sharp drainage. A mulch of grit helps keep the neck of the flower dry and reduce rain splash. Robust options include **'Clairette'** (slender petals

in blue and white), **'J.S. Dijt'** (dark purple), **'Harmony'** (bright blue) and **'Katharine Hodgkin'** (ice-blue).

Muscari / Grape hyacinth

There are several different species of muscari and increasing numbers of cultivars, but all have long-lasting, conical clusters of tiny, bell-shaped flowers from mid- to late-spring; some are fragrant. Bees love them. Most are in shades of blue or white, but there is a pink one (**'Pink Sunrise'**). *M. latifolium* (dark blue with a bright blue tip) emerges charmingly hooded by one of its leaves, and **'Grape Ice'** has a green and ice-blue tip. Other muscari to enjoy include **'Joyce Spirit'** (dark blue), **'Jenny Robinson'** (baby blue and commonly known as 'Baby's Breath') and **'Peppermint'**, which is pale blue with a green tip. As well as *M. botryoides* **'Superstar'** (bright blue), *M. armeniacum* **'Siberian Tiger'** (white) and **'Valerie Finnis'** (powder-blue). All are approximately 12–15cm.

Top left *Muscari botryoides* 'Superstar'
Top right *Iris* 'Clairette' **Bottom left** *M.* 'Joyce Spirit' with *Tulipa* 'Blue Beauty' **Bottom right** *M.* 'Jenny Robinson'

Narcissus / Daffodil

Daffodil flowering times vary enormously and it is even possible to have flowers before Christmas. The vast majority, however, flower from early to mid-spring. They do very well in pots and will tolerate shade, but may lean outwards from the shade and get broken by rain.

Daffodils are classified in myriad divisions – from trumpet and double to large-cupped and small-cupped – and it's worth exploring these as you may find a passion for a particular form. I find it more helpful to think about them as earlier and later flowering, and these are my favourites.

EARLY TO MID-SPRING

'Elka' Dainty, ivory-white, slightly twisted petals around a cool yellow corona. 20–25cm.

'Ice Baby' A miniature white daffodil with a classic trumpet shape. 15cm.

'Jetfire' Bright yellow, reflexed petals and a long orange cup; as robust as it is fiery. 20–25cm.

'Rip van Winkle' Shaggy, double, bright yellow nodding heads; an amusing character. 15–20cm.

'Spoirot' A primrose-yellow cultivar of the dwarf *N. bulbocodium* (hoop-petticoat daffodil) with a wide corona and small, narrow petals. 10–15cm.

'Tête-à-tête' A cheerful, miniature yellow daffodil of unbeatable reliability. 15cm.

'Tête Bouclé' This charming daffodil has rounded double flowers in egg-yolk-yellow. 15cm.

MID- TO LATE-SPRING

'Baby Moon' Slender leaves and stems bear clusters of tiny, bright yellow, fragrant flowers. 25cm.

'Hawera' Several small, nodding, pale yellow heads per stem with short cups and reflexed petals. Fragrant. 25cm.

'Minnow' Most stems hold two or three creamy yellow flowers with rounded petals and almost flat, lemon-yellow cups. Fragrant. 20–25cm.

'Pueblo' Vigorous, scented and productive, this multi-headed daffodil bears creamy yellow trumpets and paler petals. 30cm.

'Segovia' Small, outward-facing flowers, each with rounded white petals and almost flat, greenish-yellow cups. Very pretty. 30–40cm.

'Skype' Quite large, robust and fragrant flowers with white reflexed petals surrounding a long apricot trumpet. 35cm.

'Starlight Sensation' Multi-headed, creamy white and scented flowers open from elegant, lime-green buds. Prolific. 35cm.

Top left *Narcissus* 'Hawera' **Top right** *N.* 'Segovia' **Bottom left** *N.* 'Skype' **Bottom right** *N.* 'Starlight Sensation'

Tulipa / Tulip

When selecting tulips there are a few factors to pay attention to. Colour is of course important, but heights vary massively, from diminutive species tulips such as *T. linifolia* (10cm) to **'Blushing Lady'**, which can reach 1m. As with narcissi, tulips can be categorised into various groups, which include early-flowering and late-flowering types (across mid- to late-spring), as well as a panoply of flower shapes from the neat egg-shape of many single late tulips to the blousy forms of parrot and double tulips.

Some of the species or botanical tulips look delicate but are fairly robust in pots, although most of them don't do as well as their bigger cousins when crowded by lots of other plants. If you like these smaller forms, try *T. humilis* **'Persian Pearl'** (magenta), *T. orphanidea* **Whittallii Group** (orange and green) or *T.* **'Peppermint Stick'** (raspberry and white). Most Kaufmanniana types (such as **'Heart's Delight'**) and Greigii types (look to **'Cape Cod'**) are short in stature but have large flowers in early spring.

Choose from several different groups to get a range of heights, flower shapes and a long flowering season. You can't have too many because by spring you will be ravenous for exactly the blast of bright colour they provide. Here are a few favourites from some of the most widely available tulip groups.

Fosteriana 'Purissima' (cream-white), 'Orange Emperor'
Single early 'Candy Prince' (mauve), 'Apricot Beauty'
Double early 'Verona' (cream-yellow), 'Margarita' (magenta)
Triumph 'Prinses Irene' (orange, purple flame), 'National Velvet' (dark red)
Darwin 'Hakuun' (pure white), 'Mystic van Eijk' (peach-coral)
Lily-flowered 'Ballerina' (orange), 'Mariette' (pink)
Fringed 'Gorilla' (dark maroon), 'Honeymoon' (white)
Viridiflora 'Flaming Springgreen' (red, white, green), 'Spring Green' (white and green)
Double late 'Amazing Grace' (pink and copper), 'Antraciet' (deep crimson)
Parrot 'Apricot Parrot' (pink, green, apricot, white), 'Black Parrot' (dark maroon)
Single late 'City of Vancouver' (cream-white), 'Violet Beauty' (purple)

Top left *Tulipa* 'Prinses Irene' **Top right** *T.* 'Candy Prince' **Bottom left** *T.* 'Ballerina' **Bottom right** *T.* 'Amazing Grace'

Tender perennials

Tender perennials and shrubs need protection over winter, so all the plants in this list will need to come under cover before the first frost of autumn (unless I have specified they are borderline hardy plants, in which case they may survive if the climate in your area is forgiving). Despite the extra effort these plants require, they all make a fantastic contribution to a display for a large part of the summer, either with a succession of flowers or interesting foliage, or both.

← *Abutilon* / Abutilon

A twiggy evergreen or semi-deciduous shrub. Cultivars vary in height and habit but they all have bell-shaped flowers, commonly in warm tones. Although usually recommended for full sun, I've found that they are fine in a shady position, perhaps producing slightly fewer flowers. If you can bring them into a greenhouse they may flower well into winter. Prune weak stems in spring. Tall or lax varieties can be tied in against other wall-trained plants or a trellis, their growth is not heavy. **'Canary Bird'** (reaching 3m, pictured left) has green foliage and large yellow flowers. **'Nabob'** has dark red flowers (3m) and **'Red Tiger'** has orange flowers deeply etched with red veins (2m). **A. *megapotamicum* 'Variegatum'** has yellow flowers like

small paper lanterns held by showy red calyces and narrow green foliage splashed with gold – allow it to trail and scramble among its neighbours.

Aeonium arboreum / Houseleek tree ↑

If I had to choose just one tender succulent, this would be it. It's a tall, branching species with rosettes at the ends of its branches. It is great on its own as a sculptural statement or combined with other succulents, and because it doesn't like to be too dry for long it will even tolerate life in a mixed planting with non-succulents, as long as the light is good and it doesn't get completely covered over by other plants. If it gets tall and leggy, chop its head off and use that piece as a cutting; the main plant will re-sprout. I sometimes cut a stem and poke it into a summer planting when there is no room for rootballs, and this usually takes root while providing a bold rosette among the fluff of bedding plants. **'Zwartkop'** is one of the best black ones. It has glossy leaves and can reach 1.5m; the darkest colour is achieved in full sun (it may go a little green when under glass or on a windowsill). **'Velour'** makes softer rosettes and can become large, flushing from green to almost black in good light. **'Blushing Beauty'** (90cm, pictured on page 99) is a hybrid with *A. canariense* and is vigorous, branching and easy to look after, with green rosettes flushed with red – its colour is best in sunny conditions or when slightly stressed by drought. Before you know it you will be collecting other species and hybrids of aeonium (try tiny **'Cornish Tribute'**, variegated **'Sunburst'** or flat *A. tabuliforme*), and moving on to other succulents such as crassula, echeveria, kalanchoe...

Begonia luxurians / Palm leaf begonia →

Completely different to its tuberous cousins, this begonia has very small flowers and spectacular palmate foliage held on tall, reddish stems. It brings a tropical look to your pots and can grow to 2m.

Cuphea cyanea / Cuphea →

Its dark-eared tubular flowers have rodenty little faces so a cuphea may come in handy if you want to get children interested in gardening. One of the most eye-catching and reliable is **'Pink Mouse'** (pictured on page 138), a small (30cm) shrub with bright pink and yellow flowers. *C. llavea* (red flowers with purple 'ears', 30cm) is often sold as a bedding plant. Other cuphea species include the perennial and slightly taller *C. ignea* (narrow orange flowers, 40cm) and *C. viscosissima* (pictured opposite, top), which is a purple-flowered annual that is easy to grow from seed and which uses its extreme stickiness to scramble to 1m tall.

↙ *Fuchsia* / Fuchsia

(P) (Bo) (T) ☀ ● ◑

These shrubs, usually deciduous or semi-evergreen, are available in a wide range of habits and colours. Trailing types are useful on the edges of large mixed plantings, while more upright ones may be trained on a single stems as standards to make formal centrepieces, or just be mixed with other plants.

There are many tender varieties; one of my favourites is **'Walz Jubelteen'** (pictured bottom left), whose pink, white and green flowers face upwards and outwards instead of dangling like most fuchsias; trailing **'Trudi Davro'** (pale pink, double flowers) is also a good performer. Triphylla types such as **'Börnemann's Beste'** (salmon flowers) and **'Thalia'** (orange flowers, dark foliage) have large, handsome leaves as well as dangling clusters of flowers.

Some varieties are widely described as hardy, but really they are borderline, especially in pots. In most parts of the UK they will benefit from at least a sheltered outdoor position over winter, as even if the cold doesn't kill them completely they may be knocked right back to ground level and have to regrow, meaning you'll never get plants of a decent size. These range from tall **'Lady Boothby'** (red and purple, 3.5m with support), to **'Lottie Hobby'** (tiny pink flowers, 90cm) and *F. microphylla* **'Silver Lining'** (similar but with grey foliage, 70cm). Other tough, almost-hardy, upright fuchsias include *F. magellanica* var. *gracilis* **'Versicolor'** (red and purple flowers, variegated foliage, 1.2m), *F.* **'Checkerboard'** (red and white, 1m) and *F.* **'Lye's Unique'** (white and salmon, 60cm).

Lastly there is the minuscule (10cm), creeping *F. procumbens* and the grey-leafed version **'Wirral'**, which will happily colonise a shallow seed pan, but are best cascading from a wall pot at eye level so that you can see their tiny, upward-facing yellow flowers with green and purple sepals, red stamens and blue pollen. These are followed by outsized berries, which, like all fuchsia berries, are edible.

Melianthus major / Honey flower

This large (about 2m), woody-based perennial is borderline hardy, so give it a warm spot in a large pot and take insurance cuttings in early summer. Rather sprawling as it matures, it is worth the inconvenience for its dramatic blue-grey foliage (which smells strongly of peanut butter) and is at its best when bejewelled with early autumn dew. If happy it may produce maroon flower spikes.

Pelargonium / Pelargonium →

This is a vast genus encompassing plants that generally like full sun. As my yard is quite shady, there's a limit to how many flowers I get, but **'Crimson Unique'**, **'Paton's Unique'**, **'Quantock Candy'** and **'Voodoo'** all bloom well for me. If you use pelargoniums in mixed plantings, the more vigorous types will do best, as slow-growing cultivars are happier with a space of their own. I choose pelargoniums for their vigour and foliage (which may be scented as well as handsome) just as much as for flowers. Here are a few to look out for.

'Caroline Schmidt' A well-known zonal pelargonium, historically used for bedding schemes, so it's a tried-and-tested mixer. Clean white and green variegation, red flowers. 60cm.
'Chocolate Peppermint' Sprawling branches of fuzzy, mint-scented leaves marked with a brown blotch. It likes more water than most pelargoniums so is a useful filler in mixed plantings. 40cm.
'Crocodile' Ivy-leaved, trailing foliage with a fine network of yellow-green markings. Bright pink flowers. 25cm.
'Hederinum Variegatum' Ivy-leaved, cream margins on foliage, plus salmon-pink flowers. It is a trailing plant, so useful for the edge of a large pot or hanging basket. 30cm.
'Lady Plymouth' Deeply cut, mint-scented, grey foliage with a silvery cream edge, together with small, pale pink flowers. Its spreading habit makes it a great filler in mixed plantings, especially with pink, purple and silver colours. 30cm.

P. papilionaceum Huge, rough, oddly-scented, green leaves on a giant, fast-growing plant. Likes more fertile, moist growing conditions than many pelargoniums, so make sure it has a big pot. Bright pink, butterfly-like flowers. 1.5m or more.

P. quercifolium Slightly sticky, scented foliage that's deeply lobed and wavy with a dark central mark. Vigorous and upright, it is excellent for supporting weaker neighbours. Pale pink flowers. 60cm.

***P. × sidoides* 'Burgundy'** Small, crinkly, gently cascading, blue-grey foliage with tiny maroon flowers on long stems. 25cm.

'Radula Roseum' Deeply lobed, bright green scented leaves, plus bright red-pink flowers with dark markings. Vigorous and upright. 1m.

'Vancouver Centennial' A stellar type with pointed lobes on its bronze leaves that are edged with green. Screaming orange-red flowers. 20cm.

Top *P. × sidoides* 'Burgundy' **Middle** *P.* 'Lady Plymouth' **Bottom** *P.* 'Radula Roseum'

Plectranthus argentatus 'Silver Shield' / Silver spurflower ↑

Spreading, velvety, silver foliage grows just as well in shade as in sun, efficiently exploiting gaps among other plants. It grows up to 50cm tall, but may spread twice as far. It may also produce slender spikes of white flowers with purple buds in late summer. There are many plectranthus with attractive foliage, including upright, purple-leafed *P.* **'Mona Lavender'**, spreading, purple-backed *P. ambiguus* **'Nico'** and trailing green and white *P. madagascariensis* **'Variegata'**. It is easy to strike cuttings from all of these for plentiful plants.

Salvia / Sage →

There are annual salvias you can grow from seed, herbaceous perennials, small varieties sold as bedding plants, culinary herbs... Here I will confine myself to the perennial shrubby salvias that mainly flower after midsummer through to the first frosts of autumn. I won't get snarled up in plant taxonomy, but I have divided some of my favourites into two categories: borderline (will survive most winters outside with a bit of protection) and tender (need to come indoors for winter). The vast majority require plenty of sunshine for good flower production (but try blue-flowered *S. cacaliifolia* if your site is shady). All hate to have their roots very restricted, so be generous with the pot size.

BORDERLINE

'Amethyst Lips' Bicolour flowers that are white below and purple above. 75cm.

'Amistad' Large spikes of intense purple-blue flowers set off by black calyces. 1.2m.

S. guaranitica **'Blue Enigma'** (pictured opposite, top) Bright blue flowers. 1.2m.

S. involucrata **'Boutin'** Large spikes of vivid-pink flowers on tall, rather lax stems, which need a bit of support or winding through other plants. 1.5m.

S. × jamensis **'Sierra San Antonio'** Small, creamy pink flowers with a peach flush. 75cm.

S. **'Nachtvlinder'** This is one of the hardiest in this selection. Dark maroon flowers. 75cm.

TENDER

'Blue Butterflies' Makes up for an awkwardly horizontal habit with vivid true-blue flowers. 75cm.

S. confertiflora (pictured middle) A very large plant with bold foliage on dark stems covered in orange fuzz, plus tall spikes of fuzzy orange flowers. Splendid when back-lit by low autumn sun. 1.5m.

S. curviflora (pictured bottom) Exuberant spikes of downy magenta flowers which show up well against green foliage. 1.2m.

S. leucantha **'Purple Velvet'** Narrow grey foliage and pale stems, with arching spikes of velvety purple flowers. 1.2m.

'Phyllis' Fancy' Narrow greyish foliage, and white flowers tinged with purple. Classy. 1.2m.

Strobilanthes maculatus / Brazilian shield

Ⓟ Ⓣ

Relatively new to me, this plant has quickly become one of my favourite foliage plants for its smart, pointed green leaves marked with silvery brush strokes. The foliage is held well on fairly stiff stems which thread their way politely through other plants. Can be overwintered as a houseplant. (Pictured on page 114 with *Sanvitalia procumbens*.)

Summer bulbs

I've used the term 'bulb' pretty loosely to cover storage organs such as tubers, corms, rhizomes and even thick roots. But as all of these perennial plants die back and go dormant for the winter, they can be managed in a similar way.

Relatively hardy or borderline hardy summer bulbs can stay outside in well-drained pots in a sheltered position. I repot old lily bulbs and plant new ones while they are dormant at any time from autumn to late winter. All of the other borderline bulbs I treat more like other borderline plants (see page 138). Too much moisture is usually the enemy – a loose covering over the top of pots wintering outdoors may help to stop dormant bulbs from getting too wet. These types are generally easier to manage in pots by themselves – feed them or pot them on in spring.

The more tender ones such as dahlias and begonias can be stored dry and frost-free over winter (usually lifted when they have gone dormant and 'woken' in spring, see page 110).

HARDY / BORDERLINE

Agapanthus / African lily

As a general rule the evergreen (or semi-evergreen) agapanthus are less hardy and will best survive winter in a cool greenhouse or polytunnel, whereas deciduous varieties can stay outside in a sheltered position. All need sunshine to flower well. They are very drought tolerant but will flower poorly the following year if frequently left hungry and thirsty. Cultivars are available in many heights and shades of white and blue. Try evergreen **'Queen Mother'** (1.2m), **'Bluety'** (75cm) and **'Peter Pan'** (30cm). Deciduous varieties include **'Windsor Grey'** (1m) and **'Midnight Star'** (75cm).

Bomarea edulis / Salsilla ↗

A tuber that sends up twining stems and climbs to about 2m in a single summer. It produces coral flowers with green and yellow insides, which are very like alstroemeria, to which it is related. Exotic-looking, but surprisingly easygoing. Usually sold as a plant rather than as loose tubers.

Commelina tuberosa Coelestis Group / Dayflower Coelestis Group

Bright sky-blue flowers on leafy green stems to 90cm. The flowers close in

the afternoon. Usually sold as a plant rather than as tubers. Easy to grow from seed and may self-seed a little.

Lilium / Lily

Plant these deeply in tall pots. Watch out for lily beetle, especially if the plants are in sun (see page 149). Lilies are poisonous to cats, so don't grow them if your pet is an indiscriminate plant chewer. **'Pink Flight'** flowers generously in a shade of deep peachy pink that seems to go with anything (it has recurved petals, tolerates part shade and can reach 1.2m). Try also **'Claude Shride'** (mahogany turkscap flowers, part shade, 1m), the apricot **African Queen Group** (fragrant, trumpets, sun, 1.2m) and *L. regale* (white trumpets, an unbeatable fragrance, sun, 1.2m).

Nerine bowdenii / Bowden lily ↑

Umbels of curly flowers in bright shades of pink are produced on bare stems in early autumn. Usually sold dormant in spring, sometimes in late summer just before flowering. Plant as soon as you get it, ensuring the nose of the bulb is just above the surface, and note that new purchases may not flower in the first year. They require lots of sun and good drainage. Try the nerine/amaryllis hybrid × *Amarine tubergenii* in the **Belladiva** series (pictured above), which is more vigorous with broader petals (40cm).

Roscoea / Roscoea

All roscoeas have orchid-like flowers on top of narrow-leafed stems. The tubers are fragile, so plant carefully about 12cm deep in a tall pot and avoid disturbance; it's for this reason roscoea are usually sold already potted up. Try **R. cautleyoides** (pale yellow, 40cm), **R. purpurea** (purple, 40cm) or one of the many hybrids and colour selections such as the lovely **R. p. f. rubra** (40cm).

TENDER

Acidanthera murielae / Abyssinian gladiolus

Ⓟ 🌢 Ⓣ ☀

Fragrant, nodding white flowers reach about 90cm tall, and the inside of each one is marked with a dark central blotch. It has green, sword-like foliage. Plant groups of the corms (about 15cm below the surface) in spring in pots which are at least 30cm deep, then slot them in among other pots. The corms are best lifted, dried and stored for winter ready for planting in mid-spring. (Note that *A. murielae* is now known as *Gladiolus murielae*.)

Begonia / Begonia ↗ →

Ⓟ Ⓣ ☀ ● ◐

Tuberous begonias can be managed like dahlias (see page 110), although as their tubers sit nearer the surface I prefer to bring them in before frost hits and let them dry in their pots indoors before removing the foliage and storing the pots. They flower well in sun or in shade. Large-flowered varieties (pictured bottom right) can be very top-heavy and hard to support discreetly, but there are plenty of

small-flowered ones. **B. boliviensis** in the **Million Kisses** series, as well as **'Santa Barbara'** (white, pictured top) or **'Santa Cruz'** (bright orange) are vigorous cascaders with pendulous

flowers, and are excellent in hanging baskets or tall containers. **'Glowing Embers'** (pictured above) has orange flowers and dark green leaves that have dark red undersides (25cm), while **'Flamboyant'** is red, with rounded flowers set off by lovely bronze foliage (20cm) – both are aptly named and clump nicely to fill gaps around taller plants or fill smaller pots by themselves.

Canna / Canna ↗

Invaluable for a tropical effect, the large, bold leaves of these fast-growing plants will help to anchor your larger mixed plantings and stop them from looking too fuzzy. Repot (with the growth points near the surface) and start watering in mid-spring if you have a greenhouse or polytunnel, or

outdoors after the risk of frost has passed. Place in a sunny position for the best chance of flowers. Once you can see that the shoots are coming up fast, feed and water well for big leaves. I like the gigantic **'Musifolia'** (3m); **C. indica 'Russian Red'** is almost as tall, but not quite as overpowering, with dark leaves and (in a warm summer) orange flowers. **'Durban'** (pictured above) and **'Striata'** have colourful striped foliage and orange flowers, both reach about 1.2m. **C. × ehemanii** (2m) is elegant with green foliage and arching, coral-pink flowers. Shorter, more floriferous varieties include **'Vanilla Cream'** (tolerates part shade, 1m).

Dahlia / **Dahlia** →

ⓟ ✤ ⓣ ☀ ◗

Dahlias differ enormously in vigour, height, flower form and colour. You can plant them in pots by themselves and use them as a 'firework' plant (see page 31), though I enjoy using them in mixed plantings. Larger dahlias need a large pot and planting companions that can stand up for themselves, such as cannas or salvias, or that tolerate being overshadowed, such as plectranthus. Smaller dahlias mix well with bedding plants. Quite a few dahlias have handsome dark foliage (such as those in the **Bishop** or **Mystic** series). Research carefully, but above all have fun experimenting. Once they have begun to flower in mid- to late-summer, they keep going until the first frosts.

Start the tubers off in individual pots filled with compost in a greenhouse, covered porch or windowsill indoors in early to mid-spring; this keeps them out of the way of slugs and gives them a chance to grow robust before planting out. You can also plant tubers outdoors in pots once the risk of serious frost has passed. As greedy plants, they benefit from slow-release fertiliser at potting up and planting out, plus a high-potassium liquid feed in the growing season. Water moderately until established, then do not let them go short of moisture.

Deadheading is vital to keep the flowers coming. The buds are rounded and firm; the deadheads are much more pointed

and soft. Cut the stem just above the next node (the slight bump where the stem branches or there is a major leaf) down from the spent flower.

Once there has been a frost hard enough to blacken the foliage, cut the stems off at pot level, then tip or dig the tubers out. Remove as much compost as possible and place them upside down in empty plastic pots (with their labels). Leave them in a warm, airy place to dry, then put them in a cool, dark place for the winter. If the storage place is quite cold or very dry, cover the tubers loosely with woodshavings or crumpled newspaper. Watch out for mice, they always choose to eat your favourites!

Here are some dahlias that have repeatedly done well in my pots. There are many, many more...

TALLER (90CM–1.5M)

'Arbatax' (pictured top) Rounded flowers in white with pink petal edges.
'Bishop of Auckland' Dark red, single flowers; dark stems and foliage.
'Cornel Brons' Sturdy pompom flowers in soft orange.
'Downham Royal' Claret pompoms with a purple tinge.
'Great Silence' (pictured middle) Shades of pink flowers on long stems.
'Honka Pink' Erect, single flowers with long, pinched petals, like toy windmills.
'Ludwig Helfert' Large cactus flowers in fresh orange.
'Mexican Star' Single flowers in mahogany with a chocolatey fragrance.
'Twyning's After Eight' Single flowers in white tinged with pink; black stems and foliage.

SHORTER (45–90CM)

'Bednall Beauty' Loosely double, rich red flowers; dark foliage.
'Blue Boy' Lilac flowers on strong stems.
'Bright Eyes' Dazzling single flowers in magenta with yellow centre.
'Candy Eyes' Pale pink, single flowers; each petal has a broad central stripe of darker pink.
'Crème de Cassis' Two-tone water-lily flowers, each lilac petal is dark reddish-purple on reverse.
'Moonfire' (pictured bottom) Single flowers in yellow; dark foliage.
'Pianella' Coral-pink cactus flowers.
'Verrone's Obsidian' Dark red, single flowers with quilled petals that make a star shape.

111

Summer bedding

Summer bedding covers the plants that are available to buy in a small size in late spring/early summer, just in time to fill mixed plantings. Many are tender perennials (so you could overwinter them or take cuttings to save money the following year, see page 142), others can be grown from seed as annuals. You can buy them as plug plants by mail order in late spring, then pot them up and grow them on before planting out. Or you might think it's worth buying mature plants if you don't have room (or time) for any of these. If you want the overflowing blast of colour you see in well-grown municipal displays, you will need to have an open, light site and to feed and water regularly. My site is shady and I am not keen on using large quantities of fertiliser, so I use summer bedding plants sparingly, squeezed into the spaces between perennials.

For all plants listed: ⓟ ⓣ ☀ ◊
Anagallis monellii 'Skylover' / Blue pimpernel 'Skylover' →
Small, rich blue flowers cascade all summer long, each with a central magenta spot, which makes this plant a satisfying companion for pink- or red-flowered plants. Tolerates some shade. 20cm.

Bidens ferulifolia / Fern-leaved beggar tick
I grew this for many years and loved its small golden daisies and feathery green foliage spreading from the edge of my pots. Now there are lots of named cultivars, including **'Golden Eye'**, which has pale yellow tips to its petals. There are pink, red and orange ones too. They are fantastic for pollinators and very forgiving of occasional dryness.

Chaenostoma cordatum / Bacopa
There are many cultivars of this spreading and trailing plant, including shades of pink, white and pale blue. I like **Abunda 'Colossal Blue'** best for its large, lavender-blue flowers and fragrant greyish leaves. It spills nicely out of a mixed planting.

Dichondra argentea 'Silver Falls' / Silver nickel vine 'Silver Falls'

Silvery chains of small, rounded leaves tumble from this plant, which can be stunning on the edge of a mixed planting. I try to keep a few plants over winter as small, new ones can take a while to have enough impact (they need plenty of light). It's 10cm tall but can cascade for over 1m.

Felicia amelloides / Blue daisy

Felicia are attractive, gently spreading plants that can take a while to start producing their sky-blue daisy flowers, so I favour the variegated **'Santa Anita'** over the plain green ones to give a little more brightness to a mixed planting. Relatively easy to overwinter and to strike cuttings.

Gazania rigens / Treasure flower ↗

Bright flowers, with a sunray pattern in shades of yellow, orange and red, sitting above glossy green foliage. Flowers only open in sunshine.

Helichrysum petiolare 'Limelight' / Liquorice plant 'Limelight'

I find this gold-leaved version a little more polite than the ordinary grey-leafed *H. petiolare*, which is a vigorous, scrambling and trailing shrubby plant and can be a bit of a thug, unbalancing the composition of a mixed planting if not pruned. I use the felted foliage of 'Limelight' in sun or part shade to bring a glimmer through darker plants. There are also variegated forms.

Iresine herbstii 'Brilliantissima' / Bloodleaf 'Brilliantissima'

This isn't often sold as a bedding plant, but I'm including it in this section to prompt you to look in the houseplant section of any garden centre or nursery. It's often hard to find enough interesting foliage plants in the bedding selection because they aren't big sellers, but plenty of houseplants are happy outdoors in summer and are easily propagated. This one likes shade, and has crazily bright red and pink foliage, so use in moderation to add a bit of zing. Other varieties include the garish green and yellow **'Aureoreticulata'**.

Nemesia 'Wisley Vanilla' / Aloha 'Wisley Vanilla'

There are many beautiful colours of nemesia plants to buy and many more you can grow from seed, but the simplicity of 'Wisley Vanilla', with its crisp white flowers, each with a dab of yellow at the centre, is hard to beat. Add to this a strong, sweet vanilla fragrance and the plant is a winner. If it starts to look tired, give it a haircut and a feed. It can tolerate part shade.

Petunia / Petunia

Every year, there are more new petunias (as well as its relative surfinia and the similar calibrachoa) than you can shake a stick at (plus plenty of retirees), and their names become ever more preposterous. I like to try new ones each year because those big, round flowers are a good contrast in scale to diascia, verbena, nemesia and other summertime ditziness. Fun novelties such as **Amore 'Queen of**

Hearts' or those in the spotty **Sky** series will help to liven up a staid display. There are subtle cream and toffee colours (try × **Petchoa Beautical 'French Vanilla'**), as well as gorgeous blues. Some are deliciously fragrant.

↙ *Sanvitalia procumbens* 'Aztec Gold' / Creeping zinnia 'Aztec Gold'

A gently trailing and spreading plant with masses of tiny flowers like the sunshine symbols from a weather map. Prefers a sunny site but can do well even in constant shade. Team it with bold foliage such as *Strobilanthes maculatus* (also pictured).

Verbena 'Sissinghurst' / Vervain 'Sissinghurst'

This fine-leafed plant (still known as verbena, although the taxonomists would like us to call it glandularia) is a good threader, finding its way horizontally between other plants and popping up in random places. Other verbenas get shaded out rather easily in mixed plantings, so choose vigorous varieties such as those in the **Showboat** series, which are more upwardly spreading plants (30cm) in a wide range of colours including a sumptuous purple **'Midnight'**.

Opposite top left × *Petchoa* Beautical 'French Vanilla' **Top right** *Anagallis monellii* 'Skylover' and *Petunia* Amore 'Queen of Hearts' **Bottom left** *Verbena* 'Sissinghurst' **Bottom right** *V.* 'Midnight' and *Pelargonium* × *sidoides* 'Burgundy'

Annuals and summer plants from seed

It's easy to get carried away when you're sitting by the fire looking at all the lovely photos of brightly coloured flowers in seed catalogues, so when you feel things could get out of control try focusing on plants for pollinators – think of it as giving something back to those who enabled seed production in the first place. It's also an idea to favour climbers and taller plants because garden centres tend to stock compact versions of everything – plants that are easy to handle and transport, but which can be stumpy and boring in your pots. Growing from seed also saves a lot of money, especially if there is a filler plant you want to have in abundance.

Agastache rugosa / Korean mint →
Ⓟ 🐝 Ⓗ ☀

I haven't yet found an agastache that is not popular with pollinators. **'Little Adder'** is relatively compact (40cm), with spikes of blue flowers on strongly fragrant foliage. I also like taller **'Liquorice Blue'** (90cm). It's a short-lived perennial but you can be confident it will flower in its first summer (pictured right). May self-seed in sunny spots.

Ageratum houstonianum 'Timeless Mixed' / Mexican paintbrush 'Timeless Mixed'
Ⓐ 🐝 Ⓣ ☀

This tall (70cm) ageratum is so much more elegant and rewarding than the little blue blobs you see for sale as bedding plants. Its sprays of fluffy flowers are attractive shades of pink, blue, lavender or white.

can let these ramble among other plants too, although **Rhodochiton atrosanguineus** (purple bell vine) is a safer option for this. Sow climbers in early spring (late February to early March) to give them plenty of time to develop.

Cosmos bipinnatus / Cosmea →
Ⓐ ⚘ Ⓣ ☀

Even the taller varieties of cosmos are lovely in pots. Their fine, feathery foliage does not shade other plants out and their stems are fairly strong and can easily be given discreet support with canes. They are incredibly easy to germinate. Those in the **Cupcakes** series (pictured opposite) look charmingly like pink and white muffin cases. Try also **'Antiquity'** (for fading shades of rose and pink, 45cm), **'Xanthos'** (yellow, 60cm) and **'Apricot Lemonade'** (yellow and apricot with a pink centre, 50cm).

Hordeum jubatum / Foxtail barley
Ⓐ Ⓗ ☀

This fine, lax grass looks weedy until it flowers in late summer and becomes a wafty thing of great beauty with whiskery, red-tinged awns on fine stems up to 50cm tall, which billow in the breeze.

Cobaea scandens / Cup and saucer vine ↑
Ⓟ ⚘ Ⓣ Ⓑ☉ ☀

The king of seed-grown climbers. Purple or greenish-white cup-and-saucer bells hang on tall (easily 4–5m in one summer) stems hauled up by tendrils like tiny grappling hooks. Cobaea may be perennial in a warm site, but for pots it is best grown as an annual. Put young plants in the back of a large pot and let them romp up a sunny wall. I like the way it explores among other plants, but you can always chop heavy growth, it will have plenty to spare. Less rampant climbers that can twine and scramble up obelisks include **Thunbergia alata** (black-eyed Susan), **Ipomoea tricolor** (morning glory), **I. lobata** (Spanish flag) and **Eccremocarpus scaber** (Chilean glory flower). You

the entire plug up into a 9cm pot. Try **'Cambridge Blue'**, **'White Lady'** and **'Rosamond'** (reddish-pink). Trailing varieties include **'Monsoon'** (dark blue) and **'Sapphire'**. Plant towards the edge of the pot, though trailing varieties can be planted further back and be allowed to scramble among other plants.

Phlox drummondii / Annual phlox

'Phlox of Sheep' is worth growing for the pun alone, but it also produces clusters of simple, five-petalled flowers on 30cm stems in delicious shades of pink, cream and apricot. Try also **'Moody Blues'**, or **'Twinkle Star'**, which has madly pointed petals in pink, white, red and purple (15cm).

Lathyrus sativus var. *azureus* / Tutankhamun's pea ↑

Sadly this ornamental pea is scentless, but the sky-blue colour is sensational in early summer. It scrambles rather than climbs, so give it a low dome (about 75cm) as a support. You don't need to deadhead it (you won't be able to keep up anyway) and you can save the resulting seed for next year. It will tolerate drier conditions than *L. odoratus* (scented sweet peas).

Ricinus communis / Castor oil plant

'New Zealand Purple' is hard to beat for the dramatic impact of its large palmate foliage. The tender shrub can grow to 2m in its first season, so is usually grown as an annual. *R.* **'Blue Giant'** is a glaucous version with similar proportions. Every part, including the seeds, is highly toxic.

Lobelia erinus / Lobelia

This is widely available as a small bedding plant, but it can be easier to obtain single colours by growing from seed. Sow the tiny seeds in pinches on the surface of plug trays, and instead of pricking out individual plants pot

Senecio cineraria / Silver ragwort

Also known as *Jacobaea maritima*, you can buy this as a bedding plant, but if you want plenty of it sow seed. **'Silver Dust'** and **'Cirrus'** are good options. A happy plant can last for years in a sunny spot, reaching about 40cm.

Fruit, vegetables and herbs

I have to admit that I'm not terrifically interested in vegetable gardening. That said, I do include edible plants in my pots if they earn their place by looking good for a decent length of time. It's possible to buy fruit trees selected to tolerate long-term life in a container; these are grafted on to dwarfing rootstock to moderate their vigour and sold as 'patio' varieties. For vegetables, seed merchants often have a range of compact varieties such as dwarf French beans, bred specifically for growing in containers. The main problem with growing vegetables and fruit in pots is that many of them are less forgiving than ornamental plants and will crop very badly if you miss a watering, so it can be a commitment. For the best chance of success, grow most of them in large, deep containers so that they won't dry out too quickly. Many edible plants won't grow well if overcrowded, so your pots can look a bit sparse for a while until the crops mature. I've given a few examples here of plants that have worked among my ornamentals.

LEAVES

Many leafy crops can make a contribution in mixed plantings. Instead of growing them in rows in the veg patch, sow seed, pot up a few seedlings and grow them on for use as fillers. Try colourful **chard 'Bright Lights'**, dark and crinkly **kale** **'Nero di Toscana'**, red-leafed **beetroot 'Bull's Blood'** or **pak choi 'Red'**. For lettuce or salad leaves, it's best to sow seed directly in a trough or pot by themselves as transplanting them can make them bolt (go to seed).

TOMATOES

Tomatoes are easy to grow from seed if you can start them in a greenhouse or a sunny windowsill; alternatively buy young plants in early summer. Give them a warm, sunny spot outdoors and pay attention to regular watering and feeding. Some are bred with containers in mind. **'Tumbling Tom'** (30cm) is reliable and easy to grow. **'Maskotka'** is larger (50cm) and the bushy plants

sprawl a bit, so you may need to give it some support. These are both 'determinate' types, which means they don't need pruning. I enjoy growing the indeterminate types: for these, encourage one long main stem and pinch out any side shoots, then train them around obelisks or up canes or strings. Try varieties that look as good as they taste, such as **'Tigerella'**, **'Black Opal'** (pictured page 121) or **'Sungold'**.

CHILLIES

If you can grow tomatoes you can grow chillies. You will get the best crop in a greenhouse, but they make interesting additions to summer containers. Look for varieties recommended for outdoor use. People get very excited about the Scoville heat ratings, but I confess I usually choose them for their appearance (or their names!). My favourites are **'Black Hungarian'** (purple-tinged foliage, black fruit), **'Basket of Fire'** (yellow to red), **'Demon Red'** and **'Vampire'** (black fruit ripening to red, pictured above).

HERBS AND FRUIT

If you are a keen cook you can create a useful and beautiful herb garden in containers. I always favour the hardy perennial herbs that double as useful mixers in ornamental planting, plus I enjoy their fragrance as I garden.

Aloysia citrodora / Lemon verbena
Ⓟ Ⓣ Ⓑ☉ ☀ ◑

This deciduous shrub doesn't look very

interesting, but it smells amazing. I place it by the back door so that we get a waft of sherbet lemon every time we brush past it.

Fragaria × *ananassa* 'Pink Panda' / Strawberry 'Pink Panda'
Ⓟ ⚘ Ⓗ ☀ ◑ ◊

Strawberries can do well in even quite small containers, and it can be advantageous to raise them up out of reach of the slugs. This is a pink-flowered variety, but the white-flowered ones (such as **'Honeoye'** or **'Elsanta'**) are attractive too.

Origanum vulgare 'Aureum' / Golden oregano
Ⓟ ⚘ Ⓗ ☀ ◑ ◊

Provides a splash of sunshine among darker plants. Give it a haircut after flowering to encourage fresh growth.

Rosmarinus officinalis / Rosemary
Ⓟ 🌿 Ⓗ ☀️ 💧

Rosemary can grow to make a large shrub, so I prefer to use the prostrate forms like **'Whitewater Silver'**, which cascades from a tall pot.

Salvia officinalis **'Purpurascens'** / Purple sage
Ⓟ 🌿 Ⓗ ☀️ 💧

This sage has purple-grey leaves and reaches about 50cm. Like all shrubby salvias, it doesn't like tiny pots. Try also **'Icterina'** (bright green).

Thymus **'Silver Posie'** / Thyme 'Silver Posie' ↗
Ⓟ 🌿 Ⓗ ☀️ 💧

Pretty much any thyme is a good thyme, but this one is sturdy and shows up well all year.

Ugni molinae / Chilean guava
Ⓟ Ⓗ ☀️ ◑ 💧

Apparently this was Queen Victoria's favourite fruit. The little, dark red berries ripen in autumn and have a sweet, strawberry-like flavour. It will take clipping, so could be a pleasing subject for small topiary.

Vaccinium corymbosum / Blueberry →
Ⓟ Ⓗ ☀️ ◑

Blueberries need ericaceous compost and consistent moisture; they are one of the few cases where I place a shallow saucer under the pot in summer. Use ericaceous fertiliser and rainwater. The little pink or white flowers are

attractive, the autumn foliage is red and the berries themselves are beautiful. They fruit on the previous year's wood. Go for compact varieties such as *V.* **'Top Hat'** (50cm).

04

Care

Learn to support your plants and help them thrive

Transplanting

Gardening in containers involves moving plants about in one way or another so you need to become accustomed to transferring them from pot to pot without causing fatal damage. Transplanting is best done in spring or autumn. Transplants in high summer may struggle to establish if they keep drying out, while winter transplants that are too dormant to send out new roots may just keel over, especially if they are not quite hardy, and it's not wise to move frozen plants.

POTTING ON

As your plants develop, they may need to move into larger pots. The signs of unhappiness vary: the pot might keep drying out and falling over (meaning it is too small for the plant's watering needs); the plant's roots might be growing through the drainage holes or becoming visible at the surface; or growth and flowering have stopped. Whatever the reason, aim to move a plant out of its old pot before it begins to suffer.

• Water the plant thoroughly. This allows the plant to take up as much water as it needs, so its shoots will be less fragile and the rootball will be flexible. If you pull a dry (already stressed) plant out of a pot, its fine roots and root hairs will be clinging desperately to the pot walls and will be torn. A dry rootball will not re-wet easily in a new home, as water will flow more readily through the surrounding loose, damp compost.

• Give the rootball time to drain – leave it to do so for a few hours or a whole day. A soaking rootball can become so heavy that clumps may break off, and so soft that all the air spaces become compressed.

• Never remove a plant by grasping the stems and pulling – you are likely to break it off its roots and kill it. Always tip the pot and let gravity help; spread your fingers either side of the base of the plant to support the rootball. If there's a large enough drainage hole, push through it with your thumb or a trowel handle.

• If you need help extracting a large, well-established specimen, insert an old bread knife or a trowel around the edge of the pot to loosen the rootball from the walls. Gently tip the pot on its side (spread a groundsheet or a compost sack on the ground to catch loose compost) and slide the rootball out. Be patient because pots and plants get broken when you do this hastily.

• If a vigorous plant is pot-bound and has sent its roots circling around its old pot so that the rootball is a dense, tangled knot, new roots may struggle to emerge. In this case tease out some of the roots and loosen them

Pinch off any dead leaves and deadhead spent flowers before planting

Always water in your new plantings immediately, to help them settle in

enough to be able to explore their new home.

- Inspect the plant while potting on – now is the time to remove any dead or diseased bits and check for pests such as slugs and aphids.
- Deadheading your plant will help it to put energy it might have used for seeds into root production.
- In order to get your plant well-established, water well immediately so that its roots are quickly back in contact with water and growing medium. To settle the compost in around the roots gently, water new plantings in with a rose head attached to a watering can or with a spray. Check to ensure the compost hasn't sunk down leaving exposed roots; add more compost if necessary.

- If irrigation only ever penetrates the top few centimetres of compost, that is where most of the roots will stay. Ensure that excess water can drain out of the pot. After a really good watering, leave a new planting for at least a day or two so that the roots begin to work their way downwards, away from the drier surface.

DIVIDING

Some plants (for example mint, most bamboos) naturally creep or spread using rhizomes or stolons. These can be difficult to grow in pots as they will tend to 'run' to the edges of the container in their quest for more nutrients and world domination, and then start to decline. The run can be slowed with regular feeding,

Divide hostas in early spring when the shoots are still tightly furled

the gap with fresh compost and slow-release, high-potassium fertiliser. I treat hostas in a similar way but with a nitrogen-rich fertiliser.

STAYING PUT

It may not be practical or desirable to keep potting on vigorous or large plants. There are other options.

Root pruning Some vigorous-rooted, well-established plants are good candidates for root pruning. Many shrubs such as box can be kept in the same pot for years by removing about one third of the rootball every three or four years. I usually use my trusty bread knife to cut a slice straight down one or two sides and a few centimetres off the base. I fill the space with fresh compost and a dash of slow-release fertiliser. Do this in early spring so the plant recovers in the growing season.

Top-dressing Plants such as specimen trees and shrubs may not be good candidates for root pruning. Instead, if they are to be kept in a large pot long-term, make sure they are fed occasionally, especially when growth starts in spring. In late winter or early spring you can top-dress them. Carefully scrape away the top layer of compost or any mulch, add slow-release fertiliser and add a fresh layer of mulch or compost. Top-dressing will keep many perennials happy in the same pot for several

but to keep them happy you will need to divide the plant. Remove the plant from the pot, split it into sections and repot the sections into fresh compost. I tend to do this every two or three years (depending on the plant) and in late winter or early spring. Make sure each section has a good root system and shoots.

There is a myth that agapanthus like to be pot-bound. This is not the case. They may flower less well the year after repotting because the new space makes them concentrate on growing, but if they become very congested they will eventually stop flowering. I occasionally saw mine in half or in thirds in spring and repot, or I cut a couple of slices out like a cake, and fill years. I do the same thing with ferns and large hardy or borderline-hardy salvias.

Refreshing compost If a perennial has been in a pot for a long time but you don't have a bigger pot available, try turning it out, teasing some of the old compost away from the base and sides, and plant it back into the same pot with fresh compost and a sprinkle of slow-release fertiliser.

A note on pot washing Many people emphasise hygiene in regard to container planting, which always puzzles me as nobody attempts to sterilise a garden. I must admit that I rarely wash pots. If they still have a bit of compost or some dead leaves stuck inside I brush them out. It's rare for me to have a plant die from anything other than obvious neglect. Seedlings are more easily snuffed out by fungus so I wash out seed trays each spring with hot water and washing up liquid. I don't wash any containers with disinfectant; I think the use of disinfectant in a garden must be enormously harmful to insects, amphibians and soil fauna.

Scraping away the top layer of compost ready to add slow-release fertiliser and a fresh layer of compost

I rarely wash pots; I sometimes brush them down but I actually prefer terracotta to stay quite dirty so that it develops a nice patina

Watering

Irrigation is the subject that preoccupies container gardeners more than any other. I avoid becoming a slave to watering by putting the right plant in the right place and grouping my pots together, with the result that even in summer I do not need to water every day.

If your pots are clustered by the door, you won't forget to water them

The volume of a pot is vital to successful water management; it is a reservoir that must contain enough to support the topgrowth of the plant until the next watering. If the pot is too small you are likely to water it frequently, which may ultimately weaken the plant further. If you are watering thoroughly (not just sprinkling a little water on the surface) but still having to water every day, your plant is probably in the wrong position or the wrong pot. Try moving the pot or using a bigger one.

The rate at which the water is used depends on the plant, its stage of growth, the season, the weather and the site. You will get better at judging amounts and intervals for different plants and different parts of your site with observation and experience.

TIPS AND TRICKS

It is tempting to rush watering, particularly in summer – let's face it, it can be quite boring – but there are a few things to pay attention to.

Plants live on and around my water butts

Go steady If you pour water in too quickly or use a high-pressure nozzle on a hose, the water won't have enough time to percolate and could overflow from the top of the pot. It should have time to sink in without causing too much disturbance to the growing medium. If you are watering a medium or large pot, water at several points on the surface. If you pour all the water on to one spot, you can't expect it to spread, so move your watering can or hose around.

Water twice It is very hard to re-wet extremely dry compost. Water will bounce off it and trickle away, whereas water soaks easily into a slightly moist rootball. Sometimes it helps to give your pots a preliminary water to soften up the surface of the rootball, then to go round again and give them all a more thorough soaking. If small pots become very dry, the best way to re-wet them is to put them in a tub of water so that the water reaches about halfway up their sides, then leave them for up to a couple of hours or until the surface of the compost starts to glisten or look darker.

Gauge the volume of water I find the old adage 'water until you see it running out of the base of the pot' unhelpful, as water may leak if there is a crack between a dry, shrunken rootball and the pot. If a rootball is in a healthy condition, most of the water you give it should soak in efficiently and any

excess will trickle out later, often after a few minutes. When I water my pots with a hose I have the water running no faster than it would from a watering can and I count. If I know that a certain pot requires about half a can of water, I count to 30 or 40, which is about the time it takes me to pour that much from a can. A bigger pot may require a count of 60, a small one only 10.

Test the soil To test the compost for the Goldilocks moisture level (neither soaking wet nor bone dry) poke your finger into the compost as far as it will go. If the compost is dry, note the appearance of your plants: if the leaves appear wilted, dull or curled, remember that signal. If the compost feels moist

Small pots can be rehydrated by standing them in a tray or tub of water

then the plant is fine for a bit longer, depending on the weather forecast and your planned next watering. If, for example, the forecast is for warm or windy weather and you are away for the next couple of days, top the water up now. If the weather is calm and cool, you might be able to leave it a bit longer. Be aware that neighbouring buildings, trees and plants can all prevent rain from reaching your plants, so check for dry spots in your plantings even if the parts you can see easily seem fine.

Avoid distress Don't let your plants reach the point of distress, perhaps with yellowing leaves, wilting shoots or dropped flowers and fruit. While some plants (such as succulents) like to be on the dry side and others will forgive you for occasional neglect, many will refuse to recover after becoming too dry. If you have more than a handful of pots, identify your canary plant, that is to say the plant in your collection that is the first one to show signs of stress, like the unfortunate caged birds which used to alert coal miners to carbon monoxide.

Water early or late During summer, irrigate in the cooler part of the day, either early in the morning or late in the evening to allow the water to permeate rootballs without losing much to evaporation.

Don't overwater Overwatering, especially in cooler months, can mean

that not enough oxygen is available to the plant's roots, even causing them to rot. Not only is this a waste of time, but overwatering has implications for the environment. Please be as water wise as possible. Don't get into a blind routine of watering; stay in tune with your plants and the seasons.

Plan for holidays If your neighbours are happy to help in your absence, point out anything that might need special attention. It's prudent to group the pots a little more tightly together or to move as many as you can to a shadier position. Deadheading everything fiercely and pruning back anything that will regrow quickly will mean that less water is used by the plants for a while. Give everything a good soak just before you leave.

WATER SOURCES

As much as possible I use rainwater harvested in water butts, which is more sustainable and also preferred by many plants, especially ericaceous (lime-hating) ones in a hard water area. If you water with tap water they may eventually show signs of chlorosis (yellowing). But there are always times, especially at the height of summer, when I run out of rainwater and must use the hose.

The most useful hose fitting for watering is a lance with a head that's a bit like a small shower head. This allows you to reach into wall-mounted containers or the back of large groups of pots and it breaks the flow of water into a gentle rain, but does not spray too widely. Splashing water about is wasteful and can damage some flowers such as petunias and roses, marking them or causing them to go mouldy.

If you have a lot of containers that remain in the same place every year, you could think about an irrigation system that uses a hose and adjustable drippers inserted into the surface of the compost, though this means less flexibility and can result in dry or soggy spots, so install with care.

REDUCING WATER LOSS

Compost that isn't protected by foliage may 'cap' or form a crust on the surface, which can prevent water from percolating into the rootball. Adding a mulch of grit or gravel on the top of small and medium pots is useful. Covering any bare compost looks neat but also slows evaporation from the surface, most importantly it keeps the surface of the compost open and permeable. Add any mulch after watering in a new planting; if you add it beforehand the compost will mix with the mulch and look messy.

Keeping pots in groups reduces evaporation, but the pots at the back can be hard to reach. I sometimes place a smaller, empty terracotta pot on the surface of the pot and aim my hose into that, so that the water is funnelled to the roots. It also comes in handy when exuberant summer growth means I can't see the pot I'm trying to water (instead I can hear the water going into the little pot). There are lots of variations on the same theme: inverted plastic bottles with the ends cut off, and small pots and terracotta ollas can be embedded in containers and are particularly useful in hanging baskets and tiered planters, allowing water to reach the lower plants.

In the UK, where prolonged cool, wet weather is possible even at the height of summer, the use of saucers under pots can cause roots to rot. Shallow saucers should be used with caution, kept only for very thirsty plants and only used in summer. Do not be tempted to block drainage holes.

I harvest rainwater in butts and dustbins

SEASONAL QUIRKS

Counterintuitively, resist the temptation to automatically water plants on a hot day when you can see some of them wilting. Always check whether the roots are moist by sticking your finger in the compost. On unusually hot days plants may wilt even though they are not dry at the root, as they may be transpiring water faster than they can draw it up. Some close their stomata (pores) in hot conditions, only opening them and drawing water up when the conditions are cooler. Once the plant is shaded, wait for at least half an hour to see if it perks up before watering.

Visitors often raise an eyebrow when they see me watering my plants as black, thunderous clouds come over the horizon. If your pots are on the dry side, especially in the second half of summer when growth is voluminous, a heavy rainstorm can snap stems. This is why I do an emergency watering at least a couple of hours before heavy rain to make sure the plants are fully turgid and strong. I don't soak them, I just give them a quick, fortifying drink, prioritising the fragile ones.

During a typical UK winter you won't need to water a great deal but make sure that pots containing evergreens don't dry out completely, especially if they are in a windy position or in the rain shadow of a building. Conifers may perplex their owners by dying in spring

An empty terracotta pot can help funnel water to a hard-to-reach rootball

because they have been somewhat dry just before freezing weather and continued to lose water from their foliage without being able to draw more up from frozen compost. Conifers can be slow to wilt, so you may not notice they are suffering until they are brown and balding.

Check that pots containing spring bulbs do not dry out in late winter or early spring when their shoots are busy growing under the surface. If the compost becomes bone dry your tulips and daffodils may abort their flowers and come up blind. Don't just look at the surface of the pot; test for moisture properly by pushing your finger in as far as it will go.

Fertiliser

Plants need varying amounts of nitrogen (N), phosphorus (P) and potassium (K), plus trace elements, all of which are present in any reasonable garden soil. In a container, however, plants are unable to explore with their roots, and growing media vary a great deal in their nutrient content and ability to hold on to nutrients in the face of frequent irrigation.

Fertilisers are available as granules, controlled- or slow-release pellets and as faster-acting concentrated liquids or soluble powder for dilution.

Nitrogen (N) This encourages leafy growth and is best used in spring and early summer on plants grown mainly for their foliage (hostas, ferns). Pelleted chicken manure is an example of a slow-release fertiliser containing a relatively high proportion of nitrogen; applying this as a top-dressing in early spring is a great way to kickstart growth in plants that have overwintered in a pot. Over-use of nitrogen can cause luxuriant growth at the expense of flowers. Nitrogen is relatively soluble, so a plant in a too-small pot that needs frequent watering can run short of nitrogen quite easily, often its older leaves will discolour as it struggles to give its new shoots the nitrogen they need for healthy growth. Feeding it will help, but for longer-term results pot it on into a bigger pot.

Phosphorus (P) and potassium (K)
Phosphorus has a variety of functions in plants, including aiding healthy root growth. Potassium helps with the production of flowers and fruit, and helps plants put on tougher growth ready for winter.

General-purpose fertilisers These are formulated for flowering plants (this includes rose and tomato feeds) and are more suitable for use during summer, as they have a higher proportion of potassium. In the warmer months, when plants are growing fast, apply to keep them from running out

At the end of winter I cut back old fern fronds and top-dress with chicken manure pellets

of steam, especially those that produce a stream of flowers, such as dahlias.

Liquid feeds The advantage of liquid feeding is that it has a rapid effect; often you can see the difference in about a week or 10 days. The problem with liquid feeding is that it can be messy and wasteful, with the excess running into watercourses. To minimise waste, don't use it when your pots are very dry as too much of it will run off the surface and down the sides; make sure the compost is already damp and soft enough to soak up the liquid.

Synthetic fertilisers I am limiting my use of synthetic fertilisers as their manufacture is problematic in terms of energy consumption and emissions. Agricultural by-products such as pelleted chicken manure or alpaca manure are good slow-release options.

Vegan feeds Liquid feeds include the by-product of sugar beet production, and seaweed extract. Some people also swear by homemade nettle or comfrey tea, or liquid from wormeries. Though not strictly vegan, various fertilisers and improvers are derived from the digestate left over from anaerobic digestion (which uses food and animal waste to produce biogas).

FEEDING TIPS

- Always follow the instructions, do not make the mistake of thinking that twice as much is twice as good. Over-

Dahlia 'Crème de Cassis' needs a regular feed

fertilising can cause plants to suffer in dry conditions or to put on too much soft growth, which is vulnerable to weather and pest damage.
- I usually add a general-purpose, pelleted, slow-release fertiliser at planting time into the compost around the root zone and then use liquid feed minimally while plants are in active growth, only feeding the greediest ones or those that need a boost.
- If you have planted into fresh compost, especially if you have added a sprinkle of slow-release fertiliser, you shouldn't need additional feed for a few weeks.
- Stop feeding in late summer/early autumn, as soft, sappy growth is easily damaged by frost and the plants are slowing down. Don't get into a blind routine.

137

Hardiness

It is helpful to look at hardiness recommendations and ratings, such as the USDA hardiness zones or RHS system, which rate plants depending on their ability to tolerate conditions from tropical to -20°C.

The terms associated with hardiness tend to be hardy, frost hardy or half hardy, and tender. These can be confusing as some people consider frost-hardy plants to be ones that will take temperatures only as low as -5°C, whereas others think it means the plant is completely hardy. Meanwhile, half-hardy plants are usually not hardy at all, and are used outdoors only in the warmer months and may not tolerate temperatures below 0°C. I prefer to think of my plants in these terms:

Hardy They will survive the average UK winter.
Borderline They may suffer badly or die in a very cold or very wet winter.
Tender They will not tolerate a winter outdoors, though some plants are more tender than others.

WINTER CARE
Plants in pots are more vulnerable to winter damage: they are raised up and exposed to cold winds, their roots cannot plunge deep into the ground away from frosts and, because they are growing less actively or not at all,

poor drainage may leave them sitting in wet or stagnant compost. If you have a heated greenhouse you may be able to overwinter a lot of your tender plants. It is also worth learning some basic propagation techniques so that you can take insurance cuttings (see page 142). To find out more about dismantling mixed plantings, see page 37.

Hardy You must make sure that your winter plantings neither dry out completely nor sit in cold, sticky compost or in a pot with blocked drainage holes. Use a good-quality open-textured compost; a mulch of grit

Cuphea 'Pink Mouse' is a tender perennial and spends the winter in my heated greenhouse

can help to stop rainwater from sitting in the top of the pot around the neck of the plant.

Pot feet are widely recommended for winter plantings, but I never bother with them. I find that pots blow over more easily, freeze completely (instead of just the top) and, crucially, there is no observable improvement to drainage. I would only recommend pot feet if puddles persistently form under your pots (it doesn't do plants good to be standing in water), or if you need to avoid marking decking or paving. Make sure that pots are not standing in mud, algae or rotting leaves, as all of these can form a seal under your pots. Give the area an occasional sweep.

Freezing weather tempts you to sit indoors and read gardening books or look at seed catalogues, which is good, as you should keep your hands off your plants! Even hardy plants will be under strain in freezing conditions and will not appreciate well-meaning deadheading. Avoid moving or knocking ceramic pots, as these are easily cracked when frozen. Even if you have a greenhouse, resist the temptation to go in and out because each time lets in a blast of cold air.

If it snows, check your plants (evergreen trees and shrubs in particular). If they look laden to the point of breaking, gently shake the snow off. Do not bash them as this can

Pseudopanax 'Moa's Toes' is not quite hardy, so it is covered with fleece for the winter

damage plants whose cell walls are already struggling to cope. Don't sweep off snow lying on your pots as you are likely to damage the plants underneath. In fact, a layer of snow is a protective blanket against freezing winds. Snow in late winter and early spring provides pots with a gentle watering as it melts – ideal for the bulb shoots developing under the surface.

Borderline Many of these plants prefer to be a little on the dry side as they will be dormant or inactive in the colder months. Here in the Cotswolds (where we can get very hard frosts) I include many of the hardier fuchsias and salvias in this category. Some borderline plants, such as the more colourful phormiums, are excellent for winter structure so are worth a gamble in well-sheltered positions.

Pushing a pot against a south-facing wall or under an evergreen tree or into a porch or carport may be enough protection for a borderline plant to survive. If you have several pots, push them together because a large cluster will not freeze through as easily as a single pot. You can then cover the whole group with something breathable (fleece, shade netting, hessian or even old lace curtains) which will let a little moisture in and out. I often add old bubble wrap, carpet underlay or compost bags stuffed inside each other around the sides of these pots to insulate their roots.

If you get a period of mild weather during winter, lift the coverings and remove any foliage that has developed grey mould. When the risk of frost has passed, take off the coverings on a mild, still day and remove any dead foliage and stems. Scrape off some of the old compost, add a sprinkle of fertiliser and some fresh compost, then give plants a gentle watering to start them off again.

Tender As soon as the nights get cold and dewy and frost threatens, start to bring tender perennials you want to save for next year under cover. I start with the ones that can't stand cold combined with wet: tender succulents, zonal pelargoniums and begonias.

I bring a lot of plants into the house for the winter. This room is like a large porch with a glazed panel in the roof

(See page 110 for overwintering dahlias, which also applies to tuberous begonias.) When you bring plants under cover for the winter, check them for stowaways such as scale insect and slugs. Remove any dead/dying leaves and flowers to stop the spread of fungal disease. Take any detritus off the surface of the compost.

Some plants can become houseplants for winter: chlorophytum (spider plants), *Tradescantia fluminensis* 'Variegata' and cane begonias such as *B. rex* and *B. luxurians* are all easy to keep indoors. Most pelargoniums and tender succulents will survive on windowsills. Be very careful not to over-water, particularly in cool

Tender succulents need the lightest, frost-free position you can give them for the winter

conditions. Allow plants to dry almost completely between waterings. If your house is a little dark there are plenty of inexpensive grow lights that can help plants survive.

Deciduous plants, such as many fuchsia and *Aloysia citrodora* (lemon verbena), can be stored almost but not completely dry in a garage or shed. Check them regularly, especially when the days start to lengthen as you will need to bring them into a lighter position as soon as they show signs of life. Always wake tender plants up slowly; you must water sparingly at first, especially if they have no foliage yet to draw up the moisture.

Hardening off Be cautious returning any plants outside that have been overwintered in a greenhouse. It can

take a while for their stems and foliage to toughen up to conditions outdoors. Once the risk of frost has passed, acclimatise them to their outdoor home gradually by taking them out during the day and bringing them back in at night for a week or so. Bring them back in if the weather becomes very cold or windy.

TAKING CUTTINGS

Proficiency with taking cuttings is very useful for the container gardener. If you can make spare plants you can insure against winter losses. It also means you can afford to plant generously and can even use spare cuttings as currency, swapping plants with other gardeners. What follows are some basic instructions for taking cuttings. A bit of research will

This crate of succulents was placed in a bright position only after the plants had acclimatised to outdoor conditions in late spring

tell you the best time for taking them from various plants. I take cuttings from new spring growth to multiply my stock of plants like fuchsias and argyranthemum, and then take a lot of insurance cuttings in late summer and early autumn. Most salvias are easy to handle and easy to root, so if you are a beginner try these first.

- Fill a 9cm pot level with a roughly 60:40 mix of compost and perlite. Press the compost down to 0.5cm below the rim using the base of another pot.
- Choose healthy, new, non-flowering shoots from a well-watered plant. Cut about half a dozen, ensuring each one has three or four nodes

(leaf joints). Use the cuttings promptly, don't leave them to wilt.
- Trim each cutting just below the lowest leaf node. This is where the roots will come from. Remove the leaves from the two lower nodes without tearing the stem or leaving any stubs. If the remaining leaves are large, take more off or cut a large leaf in half. This stops the cutting from losing a lot of water before it has time to root.
- Insert the cuttings into the compost mix, spacing them evenly around the edge of the pot so that the two lower nodes are under the surface. Water well, either from below or with a fine rose. Insert a label.
- Place in a propagator at about 15ºC. If you don't have one, cover the pot with a clear plastic bag and leave on an indoor windowsill. Don't let it become dry.
- When you have a minimum of two roots poking out of the bottom of the pot, you can remove the pot of rooted cuttings, water it and put it somewhere with good light but mild temperatures to grow on a bit.
- If the cuttings were taken in spring or summer they can be potted up separately as soon as they have a few roots. If they were taken in autumn, leave them in the original pot and separate them the following spring.

Deadheading

Deadheading is one of your most important gardening duties and it's a nice, meditative job. Make sure you do the rounds of your pots at least once a week all year, nipping off flowers that have gone over (unless they are ones that will be producing seed or fruit for you). It's amazing how much better a display looks when yellowed leaves and floppy brown flowers have been taken off. Make sure you search through every hidden part of your plants, right through to the back of every pot, as doing it thoroughly keeps your plants flowering for as long as possible. Don't just strip flowerheads off: cut or pinch back to the next branch, leaf or stalk joint without leaving stubs. Winter bedding violas, pansies and daisies will all thank you for it, but don't do it when they are frozen as it can bruise them.

Snap deadheads off spring bulbs then cut stems and flopping leaves back as soon as they start to wither to keep the potful looking good. If you want to keep the bulbs and are able to move the pot out of sight, let the foliage die down naturally.

Don't give up deadheading as summer draws to a close, because taking off mushy petals and generally improving airflow around your plants will stop them from collapsing early in a heap of grey mould.

Above Deadheading violas **Opposite top** All the plants lean away from the wall of the garage; the brittle ones such as the dahlias have been staked to stop them flopping over in the rain, and the tall acacia and eucalyptus trees at the back have been tied to wires fixed to the wall **Bottom** Willow hoops form an attractive support ready for my emerging hyacinths

Support

If you put your plants and pots in the right place you shouldn't need to intervene too much, but if plants are in a pot next to the house they may lean out towards the light and fall over without a friend to lean on. Often a few twigs are enough to prop up sprawling plants such as tagetes or cornflowers. I often bend willow or hazel wands and insert them as overlapping hoops around the edge of a pot to support top-heavy flowers such as hyacinths.

In summer mixed plantings I mix sturdy, woodier plants among the more lax ones, encouraging tall floppy stems to mingle with robust neighbours, but some plants require something more substantial. I use hazel or bamboo stakes for dahlias, pushing three or four firmly around the clump just before flowering starts, adding string looped around the sticks and the whole plant. Don't truss them up too tightly: give the stems room to look natural and hide the twine by fluffing out the foliage. Remember to place an eye-protecting cane-topper on each stake.

Obelisks and domes are also useful for supporting climbers and scrambling plants or for training very tall plants such as tomatoes. Such structures have the useful side-effect of providing instant height in your display even before the plants have grown.

145

Pests and diseases

A garden where every leaf is perfect is a dead garden. If you would like the birds, butterflies and ladybirds to visit you need to take into consideration that they are all part of a complex web which includes the slugs, snails and bugs we habitually think of as the enemy. Some of these creatures also depend on weeds, so what we see as tidiness is a useless desert to most of them. I believe that we need to adjust our aesthetic ideals and relinquish a bit of control and I have found that allowing a bit of anarchy results in a balance where natural predators keep the pest species in check.

It's true that you may have to tolerate some damage while nature starts to restore a balance but it's worth it. In my professional and home gardening I have tried for many years to avoid pesticides because the unintended consequences (such as the terrible decline in our hedgehog and song thrush populations) are just too great; nowadays I don't use them at all. There are plenty of ways to avoid disastrous losses if you take time to identify and observe the species that may cause you problems.

If your plant starts to wilt, yellow or die back, before jumping to any conclusions about pests and diseases, first check whether this is a normal seasonal change. You are likely to get many of the same problems as in a normal garden, so I am only going to mention a few pests here that are very relevant to container gardening. Some pests and diseases, such as aphids and powdery mildew, are much worse if your plants are too dry and overcrowded, so you will get fewer problems if they are well-maintained.

Ants, woodlice, millipedes, centipedes and beetles These may be present, but none of them is a serious pest. Ants can be a nuisance if they nest in one of your pots because they may scoop the growing medium away from the plants' roots; they will also 'farm' aphids, harvesting the sugary honeydew they excrete and protecting them from predators. They really only do this in pots that are too dry and have been undisturbed for a long time. They will usually stay out of well-watered (remember this means thoroughly rather than frequently) pots. If watering doesn't shift them you can simply disturb them by emptying the pot – often if you leave the rootball exposed for an hour or two the ants will move house and/or be eaten by birds and you can pop the rootball back in.

Woodlice and millipedes are scavengers, almost always eating dead and decaying material. If your plants are healthy and growing well they are unlikely to be affected. Centipedes (flatter and faster than millipedes) are predators, doing no harm to plants, as are the vast majority of beetles. Please don't kill anything unless you are absolutely sure it is a pest and doing serious damage, as you will be removing important food for birds, hedgehogs and amphibians.

Slugs and snails Damage ranges from nibbled flowers to overnight obliteration of newly planted seedlings and gaping holes in foliage. Encourage natural predators (birds, frogs, toads, hedgehogs) and don't position vulnerable plants such as hostas in snail hotspots (next to walls or where smooth leaves form a bridge into the pot). When

planting a pot check for hitchhikers before you settle plants in; a small slug or snail hidden under a leaf will thank you for giving it a lift, and when it gets big enough it will find the soft compost a great place to lay eggs.

If you notice slug or snail damage check inside the rim of the pot, or if the rim is curved over check underneath it, as snails will roost around rims during the day. Slugs tend to hide under foliage or underneath the bottom of the pot, often tucked into the drainage hole. Some people recommend going out at night with a torch to find them as they crawl about but I prefer to look on a dry day, when they will be conserving moisture and hiding in these predictable places.

The yellow hosta is not dead, it's resting; try to enjoy a plant's seasonal ups and downs

Garden snails love to lay their eggs in compost; if you find them, you can give them to the birds

I never lift any pot without checking underneath it for slugs. I don't bother with barriers such as wool pellets, copper tape or smearing grease on the rims of pots because these barriers are so easily bridged by foliage.

Slugs and snails will follow their own slime trails back to your plants each night, so you really can make a difference by checking for and removing the little blighters every now and then. I retire them to the compost heap, where they can make themselves useful.

If you have a lot of trouble with slugs and snails and can't work out where they are coming from, you can try using nematodes, which are available by mail order; you water these on when the conditions are warm and damp, and if you follow the packet instructions carefully you can make a big dent in the population.

Vine weevils Dull brown adults (they are all female and march around like little, egg-laying machines) eat irregular notches in the edges of some foliage but the most important damage is caused by the larvae (c-shaped, about 1cm long, white with a brown head), which hatch in the compost and feed on the roots of plants. You often won't notice there's a problem until your plant dies. This damage tends to be worst in spring and autumn. Keep an eye on vulnerable plants (succulents, primulas and anything in the saxifrage

Lily beetles This is a bright red beetle, black underneath, which falls on its back when disturbed and often squeaks when you pick it up. The larvae do enormous damage to lilies and fritillaries. Repot these bulbs in fresh compost between autumn and early spring to get rid of overwintering adults. In spring and early summer remove the eggs, which are bright red and glued in groups underneath the leaves. If you later find larvae (camouflaged by their own excrement) eating the foliage, wash them off with a jet of water. Don't squash any beetles indiscriminately – there are lots of beneficial ones.

Rodents Mice and squirrels can be a problem if they discover your pots, especially if they have a taste for spring bulbs. My local mice love crocus corms. I have found that the best deterrent is keeping pots near the house and mulching vulnerable ones with 2–3cm of grit or pebbles.

family, especially heucheras); often you can rescue them if you notice that they have stopped growing or have come loose. I spread affected compost thinly on the ground so that the birds can eat the grubs. Wash the compost off the remaining roots of affected plants (and even off the roots of newly bought vulnerable plants) and repot, or use what's left of your plant as cuttings. A grit mulch around succulents seems to reduce the number of eggs laid in those pots. Nematodes are available.

Opposite top Slugs like to hide in drainage holes **Middle** Adult lily beetle **Bottom** Margery on patrol **Above** A little leaf damage on hostas isn't the end of the world

Weeds

A friend once proudly presented me with a young potted plant that she had grown from a packet of geranium seed. It looked healthy and I thanked her profusely, not liking to point out that she had carefully potted up a thistle which had blown in from the fields next to her garden. For me, pretty much any happy plant is beautiful and I am content to let weeds colonise the cracks in my yard, but I draw the line at cosseting them in my pots to the detriment of the plants that I have chosen. When it comes to weeds it pays to know your seedlings so that you can remove thistles, dandelions or meadowgrass from your pots promptly before they become too established to remove without damaging other plants.

There's a fine line between welcome self-sowers and weeds, so you need to judge where that is. I find Welsh poppies beautiful unless one is growing in the centre of a more delicate plant, in which case I take it out while young. I also enjoy getting little presents from birds and mice, such as cotoneaster seedlings. One year a very diligent mouse sowed a sunflower in almost every pot.

If you are using proprietary compost you shouldn't get too many weed seedlings popping up in your pots but they can be brought in on the compost of the potted plants that you buy. A sprinkling of weed seedlings doesn't usually worry me but I avoid buying plants badly infested with *Cardamine hirsuta* (hairy bittercress), which matures in no time and its seeds ping out of the pods as soon as you touch it. *Oxalis corniculata* (creeping woodsorrel) is worse – its seed capsules are even more explosive. Cardamine is easy to pull out and if you do it before the seeds have set that is an end of the matter, but oxalis is a wiry-rooted perennial and sneakily regrows from any small part you leave behind.

Mosses and liverworts sometimes colonise the top of a rootball, especially one that has been sitting undisturbed in damp, shady conditions. I rather like the look of moss and have been known to add it around the base of a tree or shrub, but liverwort can be a nuisance, forming an almost impermeable mat on the surface of the pot. I normally just peel it off and either top up with fresh compost or add a grit mulch, which stops it from regrowing.

Opposite I don't mind the weeds that colonise the cracks and gravel in my yard; sometimes useful plants seed themselves there as well

Page numbers in *italics* indicate an illustration.

Resources

I am not going to give a long list of resources because I would like to encourage you to shop as locally as possible. For readers in the UK, these are my brief suggestions. For plants, the **Independent Plant Nurseries Guide** is a good place to start (independentplantnurseriesguide.uk). Look out also for plant fairs near you, such as those run by **Rare Plant Fairs** (rareplantfair.co.uk). For inspiration, visit local gardens, especially via the **National Garden Scheme** – some of the smallest gardens have the best container ideas (ngs.org.uk). Then get yourself on **Instagram** where gardeners like me are waiting to share plant combinations and practical tips.

A note on plant names

Do note that botanical plant names and even varieties can have at least one synonym – an alternative which has more or less equal value to its given name. Some names change over time as botanists and taxonomists find out more about the plants or where precedents are flagged. We have tried to be as up-to-date as possible, but where a plant has several names available, we have favoured the one that is most familiar to the average home gardener and under which the plant is most readily found for sale in the UK (even if botanical experts may not agree). We have treated trade names as cultivar/variety names (listed between single quotation marks) even though these should technically be shown in a different typeface. We have used some common names (such as hazel, rather than *Corylus avellana*) in parts of the book. All of these decisions have been made for ease of use.

Acknowledgments

I would like to thank my brilliant and always supportive husband Chris and my sons Peter and Alexander who have all been neglected in favour of plants, but encourage me nevertheless. Also a huge thanks to Zena Alkayat, commissioning editor, Sarah Pyke, designer, and to Andrew Maybury, photographer and cat-wrangler extraordinaire – all of you made the creation of this book a happy and calm experience, each bringing your own flair and creativity.

First published in 2022 by Frances Lincoln
an imprint of The Quarto Group.
The Old Brewery, 6 Blundell Street,
London, N7 9BH, United Kingdom
www.Quarto.com

gardening · nature · inspiration

A Bloom book for Frances Lincoln
Bloom is an independent publisher for gardeners, plant admirers,
nature lovers and outdoor adventurers. Alongside books and stationery,
we publish a seasonal print magazine that brings together expert
gardening advice and creative explorations of the natural world.
Bloom celebrates all green spaces, from wilderness to windowsills,
and inspires everyone to bring more nature into their lives.
www.bloommag.co.uk | @bloom_the_magazine

Text © 2022 Harriet Rycroft
Photography © 2022 Andrew Maybury
Illustrations © Botanical line art sketches by Madiwaso via Creative Market

Commissioning editor Zena Alkayat
Designer Sarah Pyke
Photographer Andrew Maybury
Proofreader Joanna Chisholm
Indexer Michèle Clarke

A catalogue record for this book is available from the British Library.

ISBN 978-0-7112-7248-4

Printed in China

MIX
Paper from
responsible sources
FSC
www.fsc.org   FSC® C016973